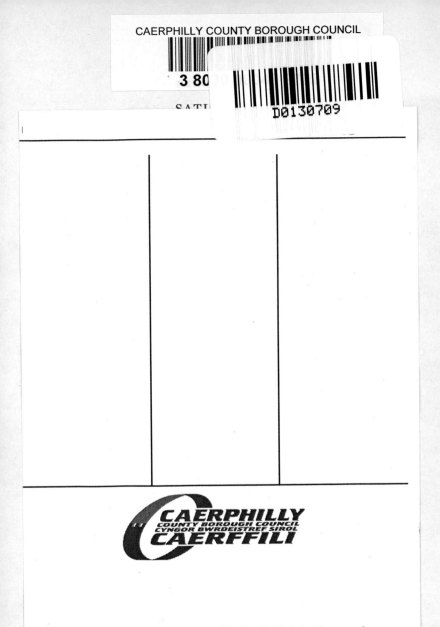

**Please return / renew this item by the last date shown above**

Dychwelwch / Adnewyddwch erbyn y dyddiad olaf y nodir yma

PENGUIN BOOKS

NONFICTION

Ammon Shea has been reading dictionaries for twenty years. Along the way he has supported this habit by being a street musician in Paris, a gondolier in San Diego and a furniture mover in New York City. He lives in New York with his girlfriend (a former lexicographer) and a large number of old dictionaries. Visit his website at www.ammonshea.com.

# *Satisdiction*

*One man's journey into all
the words he'll ever need*

A M M O N   S H E A

PENGUIN BOOKS

PENGUIN BOOKS

Published by the Penguin Group
Penguin Books Ltd, 80 Strand, London WC2R 0RL, England
Penguin Group (USA) Inc., 375 Hudson Street, New York, New York 10014, USA
Penguin Group (Canada), 90 Eglinton Avenue East, Suite 700, Toronto, Ontario, Canada M4P 2Y3
(a division of Pearson Penguin Canada Inc.)
Penguin Ireland, 25 St Stephen's Green, Dublin 2, Ireland (a division of Penguin Books Ltd)
Penguin Group (Australia), 250 Camberwell Road, Camberwell, Victoria 3124, Australia
(a division of Pearson Australia Group Pty Ltd)
Penguin Books India Pvt Ltd, 11 Community Centre, Panchsheel Park, New Delhi – 110 017, India
Penguin Group (NZ), 67 Apollo Drive, Rosedale, North Shore 0632, New Zealand
(a division of Pearson New Zealand Ltd)
Penguin Books (South Africa) (Pty) Ltd, 24 Sturdee Avenue, Rosebank, Johannesburg 2196, South Africa

Penguin Books Ltd, Registered Offices: 80 Strand, London WC2R 0RL, England

www.penguin.com

First published in the United States as *Reading the OED* by Perigee,
a member of the Penguin Group (USA) Inc., 2008
First published in Great Britain as *Reading the Oxford English Dictionary* by Allen Lane 2008
Published in Penguin Books with a new Afterword as *Satisdiction* 2010

1

Copyright © Ammon Shea, 2008, 2010
All rights reserved

The moral right of the author has been asserted

Text design by Ellen M. Lucaire

This book describes the real experiences of real people. The author has disguised the identities
of some, and in some instances created composite characters, but none of these changes has
affected the truthfulness and accuracy of his story.

Printed in England by Clays Ltd, St Ives plc

978-0-141-04025-7

www.greenpenguin.co.uk

*For Alix, who helps me define the world*

# Acknowledgments

*Jim Rutman, a great literary agent who not only did not
laugh at me when I first proposed the idea, but instead spent
an inordinate amount of time helping me make it better.*

*Marian Lizzi, simply everything an editor
should be, and a joy to work with.*

*Katie Wasilewski, helpful and gracious
above and beyond the call of duty.*

*Charlotte Brewer, Peter Gilliver, Jesse Sheidlower, and all
the other members of the Dictionary Society of North America who
had the patience and inclination to answer my questions.*

> The dictionary is never consulted in its entirety.
> Henri Béjoint, *Tradition and Innovation*
> *in Modern English Dictionaries*

# Exordium

### (Introduction)

THERE ARE SOME GREAT WORDS in the *Oxford English Dictionary*. Words that are descriptive, intriguing, and funny. Words like *artolater* (a worshipper of bread). It is unlikely you have ever seen *artolater* written or heard it used in speech, as it hasn't been used much since the seventeenth century. It is in the *OED*, but even if you own this magnificent dictionary it is still highly improbable that you have ever seen this word.

In fact, if you were to open the *OED* at random, there is about a .0046 percent chance that the page you are looking at will have *artolater* on it. This is approximately equal to the chance that your child will become a professional athlete.

If you were to sit down and force yourself to read the whole thing over the course of several months, three things would likely happen: you would learn a great number of new words, your eyesight would suffer considerably, and your mind would most definitely slip a notch. Reading it is roughly the equivalent of reading the King James Bible in its entirety every day for two and a half months or reading a whole John Grisham novel every day for more than a year. One would have to be mad to seriously consider such an undertaking. I took on the project with great excitement.

SOME PEOPLE COLLECT MATCHBOX CARS or comic books. Others collect more obviously valuable things, such as rare paintings or cars. Most of these collections are made up of tangible objects, things to which one can assign some sort of monetary value.

I collect words.

One could also say that I collect word books, since by last count I have about a thousand volumes of dictionaries, thesauri, and assorted glossaries, but I don't see that as a collection. These books are merely the tools with which I gather my collection. Although the books may be physical objects that take up room in my apartment, the real collection is the one that takes up all the room in my head, providing me with endless fascination and amusement as I move through the day, constantly thinking "There's a word for that. . . ."

I do not collect these words because I want to impress friends and colleagues with my erudition. For most of the past ten years while I have been reading dictionaries and collecting words I've been employed as a furniture mover in New York, and the words

# Exordium

I've learned in old dictionaries would be, to put it mildly, singularly inapplicable in that milieu. My friends know that I read dictionaries for fun, and have come to accept this proclivity with relative good grace, but they are not terribly interested in or impressed by my word collection. My girlfriend, Alix, used to be a lexicographer for Merriam-Webster, and she has a considerably greater interest in my word collection than any normal person would (not registering even the slightest complaint when I brought along several walls' worth of dusty and shedding dictionaries when I moved in with her). But sometimes I have a sneaking suspicion that she gets slightly irritated, such as when I point out that *philoprogeneity* and *philostorgy* both refer to a parent's love for his or her child. When I asked her about this recently she said, "The point at which I became bored has long since passed." I've chosen to interpret this as a good thing.

As far as hobbies go, it is as most of them are—largely useless. Contrary to what many self-help books would have you believe, adding a great number of obscure words to your vocabulary will not help you advance in the world. You will not gain new friends through this kind of endeavor, nor will it help you in the workplace. At best you might bore your friends and employers, and at worst you will alienate them, or leave them thinking that there is something a little bit wrong with you.

I read my first dictionary, *Webster's New International* (aka *Webster's Second*), published in 1934, almost ten years ago. I can close my eyes and remember exactly the way the pages smelled, their delicately yellowish tint, and the way they would easily tear if I turned one too eagerly. After several months, many headaches, and a great deal of coffee, I'd made it from *a* to *zyzzogeton* (a large South American leaf hopper). My head was so full of words that I often had trouble forming simple sentences out loud, and my speech became a curious jumble of obscure words and improper syntax. It felt wonderful, so I went out and bought the sequel, *Webster's Third New International.*

I've been reading dictionaries, lexicons, and glossaries ever since. I have read archaic and provincial dictionaries, dictionaries of slang and colloquialisms, and dictionaries of medical and psychiatric terms. The reading of every one is a delightful mix of comfort and anticipation, as I find both words I remember fondly and words I have never seen before.

Some people find it odd that I take such pleasure in an activity that is so inherently Sisyphean. Of course, I don't find it odd at all: think about your favorite book, and how endlessly satisfying it would be if that book never really ended. The dictionary is my favorite book, and even if I did one day manage to read all the way through every dictionary and word book I own, I could always go back to the beginning and start again. It's certain that by that point I will have forgotten enough of what I've already read to make it just as interesting as the first time through.

I HAD BEEN MEANING TO READ the *OED* for years, but I always found some way to put it off. My reasons were twofold: (1) if I read it I wouldn't have it to look forward to, and (2) its length and exhaustive nature were intimidating, even to this veteran reader of dictionaries. There is quite a lot of text in those twenty volumes, and I knew that reading through it all would require a fairly serious commitment of time and focus. I would hate to read all the way through to the letter *N* and then abandon ship, relegating myself to the status of "that guy who read halfway through the *OED*."

But these are not legitimate reasons to avoid reading a book, and so I came to the decision to begin reading this dictionary. As I read I jotted down all the words I found outrageous, funny, or archaic and deserving of resurrection. The book in your hands contains all the words from the *OED* that I think people would like to know about, if only they didn't have to read the whole damn dictionary in order to find them.

I will admit that there was another reason I initially avoided reading the *OED*: I was leery that it would be a very serious work full of very serious words, and dreadfully unfunny to boot. This quickly proved not to be the case. Make no mistake, the *OED* is an enormously scholarly work—but that does not mean it is not also entertaining and wonderfully engaging. Who can resist a book that uses words like *all-overish* (having a general and indefinite sense of illness pervading the body)? And it is hard to be too intimidated by any book that uses a word such as *assy* (asinine).

The *OED*, more so than any other dictionary, encompasses the entire history of the modern English language. By so doing it also encompasses all of English's glories and foibles, the grand concepts and whimsical conceits that make our language what it is today. In just the first letter of the *OED* you will find words as magnificent as *agathokakological* (composed of good and evil), as delicately shaded as *addubitation* (the suggestion of doubt), and as odd as *antithalian* (opposed to fun or festivity).

I view *Satisdiction* as the thinking person's CliffsNotes to the greatest dictionary in the world. It is also an account of the pain, headache, and loss of sanity that comes from spending months and months searching through this mammoth and formidable dictionary—and pulling together all of its most beautiful and re-markable words.

If you are interested in vocabulary that is both spectacularly useful and beautifully useless, read on, and enjoy the efforts of a man who is in love with words. I have read the *OED* so that you don't have to.

# A Note on the Entries

ALL OF THE WORDS DEFINED in this book come from the second edition of the *Oxford English Dictionary*, published in 1989 by Oxford University Press. Unless otherwise specified, the definitions provided for these words come from me. Any mistakes, unless otherwise specified, also come from me.

The words included here are not necessarily intended to be used as defined. In many cases the words have been obsolete for hundreds of years. In other cases I have listed one meaning (out of several possible ones), and it is not always the primary meaning of the word.

I have not included a pronunciation guide for the entries, for several reasons. The *OED* does not explain how to pronounce words that have not been in common use for hundreds of years for the simple and very good reason that the editors do not know how the words are pronounced. I certainly do not know either,

# A Note on the Entries

and it would be extremely presumptuous for me to hazard a guess.

I find that I enjoy these words as curios rather than new words to use in daily conversation, contenting myself with the fact that such strange and lovely words exist at all. Perhaps you'll feel differently and will want to sprinkle them into your vocabulary, to impress or amuse. That's fine—they surely won't go unappreciated. Or let them dance silently in your head as you pass through the day. It matters not, so long as you enjoy them.

# A

M**Y** *OXFORD ENGLISH DICTIONARY* arrives at 9:27 one Monday morning, brought by a deliveryman who is much cheerier than I would have expected anyone carrying 150 pounds of books up a flight of stairs to be. Five boxes, containing twenty books that promise to take up the next twelve months of my life.

I rarely buy books that are brand-new, and so I feel almost nervous as I take them out and begin removing them in their pristine condition from the plastic wraps. They have a decidedly new-book smell, a scent far more intoxicating to me than that of a new car. After all, you cannot read a car. Of course, I think old books smell just as good as new ones. I arrange them, in order, on the floor along one wall in my living room. They are all dust-jacketed in dark blue, with a regal and chitinous gloss, resembling the covering of some beautiful and wordy beetle.

I sit in an armchair across the room and just stare at them for some minutes. It seems to me that they are glowering on the floor, so I get up and begin making room on the bookshelves. I take a twelve-volume set of the *Century Dictionary* down and unceremoniously move it to the closet. Then I shuffle a few copies of *Webster's Third* around and place a number of other items on their sides and a few more on whatever surfaces I can find. After about fifteen minutes of arranging, compressing, and stacking books, I've made enough room to put nineteen of the twenty volumes of the *OED* away. I leave the first one (*A–Bazouki*) by the armchair and go to make myself a strong cup of coffee. I drink the coffee and then sit down to begin reading.

Almost immediately the simultaneous pleasures and frustrations of dictionary reading become apparent again. First and foremost, the *OED* is a great read. The definitions are usually beautifully written and there is a palpable sense of the massive amount of human thought and learning that was required to put this work together. The history of English seeps into your head as you read through not just the words and their definitions, but also their etymologies and the ways in which they have been used by writers over the centuries.

I find myself subject to the entire range of emotions and reactions that a great book will call forth from its reader. I chuckle, laugh out loud, smile wistfully, cringe, widen my eyes in surprise, and even feel sadness—all from the neatly ordered rows of words and their explanations. All of the human emotions and experiences are right there in this dictionary, just as they would be in any fine work of literature. They just happen to be alphabetized.

I keep paper and pen by my chair so that I can write down the things in the dictionary that I find interesting. After the first hour I realize that I've been writing down far too much, and that if I continue taking notes at this rate I'll never finish reading. But there is just so much in the dictionary that I wish were in my head, and I read with the constant knowledge that I'm passing by things that later I'll want to know. The answers to questions that I've had for years and the answers to questions that I never knew I had are coming up constantly.

These are some of the pleasures of reading the dictionary, and they are indeed sublime. The frustrations are considerably more pedestrian. After the first three hours of reading I have the kind of headache that makes life feel unfair. It is a pounding that keeps pace with my heartbeat, as though I had a second heart, located in the lower-left back part of my head, the sole purpose of which is to pump tiny spasms of pain, rather than blood.

I see better out of my left eye than my right, and I spend so much time squinting as I read that I find myself squinting at other times as well. The *OED* uses different typefaces for different things: the headwords are written in bold, the definitions are in a regular font, the etymologies are in some sort of italicized shorthand, and the citations are written in a smaller type than the rest. Having to constantly make adjustments in my vision, albeit minor ones, is one of the main causes of the headaches.

All day long I'm plagued by the feeling that I can't quite remember a word. This is the first thought in my head every morning when I wake. It is often the last thing I think about before I fall asleep.

I read for eight or ten hours each day. Sometimes it is meditative, and my reading assumes a pleasant rhythm for long stretches. At other times it feels maddeningly dull, and I suddenly realize that for the past hour I've been scanning pages with my eyes but not really reading anything at all, and have to go back to where I lost attention. Somewhere in the neighborhood of *avenge* I have an alarming spell when my vision suddenly turns gray and stays that way for several hours. I find myself doubting this somewhat absurd enterprise, and wonder whether it really is worth reading the whole thing.

I remind myself of the marvelous reply that the British mountaineer George Mallory gave to the *New York Times* in 1923 when asked why he wanted to climb Mount Everest: "Because it's there." Unfortunately, Mallory died during his attempt to climb the mountain, and while I have no illusions that my attempt will be nearly as perilous or dramatic as his, I can sympathize with his reasoning. The nineteen remaining volumes of the *OED* are there, sitting on my bookshelves, and if I give up reading now I know that I will forever wonder what is in them.

After my vision returns to normal I decide that what I need is a magnifying glass. I dig out the magnifier that comes with the compact edition of the *OED* (the malicious version that has four pages of text condensed on each page of paper) and begin reading again. It does not work as I intended it to. Its partial success at magnifying the text pales in comparison to its complete success in bringing back my headaches and squints.

My friend Peter suggests that I buy myself an overhead projector, so I can put a screen up on the wall and read the books on it. This is a tremendously appealing thought, and I imagine myself reading the *OED* as if it were a movie. But when I look into getting one I find that the affordable models require one to place the book facedown on the machine, meaning that I would have to pick the book up and turn it over, flip a page, and then place it back down—more than ten thousand times. This seems impractical.

I reluctantly decide that the *OED* is meant to be read unencumbered by technology. And so that is how I read it, helped along by a cup of espresso once every hour or so. After eight days, when I finally reach *azymous* (adj.—unleavened), I feel a shiver of pleasure and relief; not because I think it an interesting word, but because it is the last word in *A*, which means I am starting to make some progress.


## Abluvion *(n.) Substance or things that are washed away.*

Chances are you have never stared at the dirty bathwater washing down the drain and wondered, Is there a word for that? but now you will forever be cursed with the knowledge that indeed there is.
*also see:* illutible

**Accismus** (*n.*) *An insincere refusal of a thing that is desired.*

As in: "No, please, I really would like for you to have the last donut."

**Acnestis** (*n.*) *On an animal, the point of the back that lies between the shoulders and the lower back, which cannot be reached to be scratched.*

I am very glad I found this word early in my reading of the *OED*—the fact that there existed a word for this thing which previously I had been sure lacked a name was such a delight to me that suddenly the whole idea of reading the dictionary seemed utterly reasonable.

*also see:* onomatomania

**Addubitation** (*n.*) *A suggestion of doubt.*

My favorite kinds of words are not the grand and dramatic creations. Nor are they the short and brutish words that make up so much of our everyday speech. More than any others I love words like *addubitation*, words that describe a phenomenon about which you never even wondered.

**Admurmuration** (*n.*) *An act of murmuring.*

This word describes a recognizable phenomenon, as of the low roar of voices in between points at a tennis match. The *OED* notes that this word was "never used"—only having appeared in prior dictionaries—and thus its retention might be considered more hopeful on the editors' part than lexicographic.

A

## Advesperate *(v.) To approach evening.*

For all intents and purposes this word is almost useless, for I doubt that anyone will ever use it in conversation with me, and I fervently hope that I myself am never prone to utterances such as "Let's hurry! It's *advesperating*!" Nevertheless, this word brings me a great deal of pleasure, as occasionally when I am walking down the street and the light of day is about to change to the light of early evening, the word will flit through my mind, and I have a rush of joy from knowing how to name such an ephemeral moment.

## Advocitate *(v.) To call upon frequently.*

The secret and inescapable fear of unstudied schoolchildren the world over—that they will be *advocitated*.

## Aeipathy *(n.) "Continued passion." (John Craig, A New Universal . . . Dictionary of the English Language, 1847)*

Although John Craig does indeed define this medical term thusly, I should point out that his is not the only definition listed in the *OED*, and also that *passion* did not always have the same meaning that it does today. The *OED* also states that Robert Mayne's *Expository Lexicon* of 1853 defines this word as a "term for an unyielding or inveterate disease." It is unclear to me whether this discrepancy is due to Craig using the word *passion* in an antiquated sense or because Mayne thought of love as a sickness.

*also see:* resentient, unlove

## Aerumnous *(adj.) Full of trouble.*

More descriptive than *troublesome*, and with far more gravitas than *irksome*, *aerumnous* is practically begging to be reintroduced to our vocabulary. It describes everything from your squalling children to the used car that your wife's brother managed to sell you last year.

## Agathokakological *(adj.) Made up of both good and evil.*

*Agathokakological* is an imposing and meaty word. Don't be scared of it; you don't have to use it in casual conversation. Sometimes it's enough to merely know that a word exists in order to enjoy it.

*also see:* jocoserious

## Agelastic *(n.) A person who never laughs.*

Grim, but with fewer wrinkles.

*also see:* cachinnator, hypergelast

## Agerasia *(n.) A lack of the signs of age; a youthful old age.*

Many words in English have a similar meaning to *agerasia*; however, this is one of the few that does not seem to have any connotations of childishness or immaturity attached to it.

## Airling *(n.) A person who is both young and thoughtless.*

Although it might well seem redundant to specify a person as both young and thoughtless (how many words do you know for one who is young and thoughtful?), *airling* does us the favor of employing a certain amount of both gracefulness and economy.

**All-overish** *(adj.) Feeling an undefined sense of unwell that extends to the whole body.*

It is rare that we are presented with a word simultaneously so vague and so useful. The next time you call in sick to work because you simply do not feel like going, *all-overish* presents the perfect description for what is ailing you.

**Ambidexter** *(n.) A person who accepts bribes from both sides.*

To be perfectly fair to *ambidexter*, this definition is not the only one the *OED* lists. *Ambidexter* also refers to a person who is unusually dextrous, or who is two-faced in a general sense. However, the earliest instance of the word, in a book from 1532 titled *Use of Dice Play*, employs it to mean "one who takes bribes indiscriminately."

**Ambisinistrous** *(adj.) Having two left hands; clumsy.*

This word is more or less the opposite of *ambidextrous* (which has as its etymological root "two right hands").

**Anonymuncule** *(n.) An anonymous, small-time writer.*

This delightful word is the result of combining *anonymous* with the Latin word *homunculus* ("little man").
*also see:* bully-scribbler

**Anpeyn** (*v.*) *To exert a great deal of effort; to try one's hardest.*
Much more evocative than *strain, strive,* or *struggle.*

**Antapology** (*n.*) *A response or reply to an apology.*
*Antapologies* come in two flavors: gracious acceptance and self-righteous fury.

**Antinomian** (*n.*) *A person who claims that moral law has no authority over Christians.*
A number of sects have espoused *antinomianism* over the years, but this word, as listed in the *OED*, specifically refers to one that formed in Germany in 1535, which purportedly held the view that under the "law of grace" its members were exempt from moral law.
*also see:* misdevout

**Antipelargy** (*n.*) *"The reciprocal love of children to their parents." (Thomas Blount, Glossographia, 1656)*
An idealistic word. While there is a similar word for the love that parents feel for their children (*storge*), there is, to the best of my knowledge, no word to describe the irritation that either parents or children feel for the other.
*also see:* storge

**Anti-rumour** (*v.*) *To raise an opposing rumor.*
Ah, the contrary rumor. Many, if not most of us, like to think

that we'd gracefully turn the other cheek upon discovering that we're the subject of some nasty and scurrilous rumor. Perhaps we'd shake our head a bit sadly and murmur something philosophical in French. This is rot; most of us will immediately try to come up with an anti-rumour that is far worse than the one spread about us.

*also see:* countercozen

## Antisocordist *(n.) An opponent of laziness or idiocy.*

Along with cleaner of the Aegean stables and high school English teacher, being an *antisocordist* is one of the most thankless and hopeless jobs available. It invites comparison with another word that comes up slightly later in the alphabet, *futilitarian*—one who is devoted to futility.

## Antithalian *(adj.) Opposed to fun or merriment.*

Taken from *anti-* and *Thalia*, the Greek muse of comedy. May be applied with equal facility to any number of institutions or individuals one comes across in life.

## Apricity *(n.) The warmth of the sun in winter.*

A strange and lovely word. The *OED* does not give any citation for its use except for Henry Cockeram's 1623 *English Dictionarie*. Not to be confused with *apricate* (to bask in the sun), although both come from the Latin *apricus*, meaning exposed to the sun.

## Arrision (n.) *The action of smiling at.*

I don't know why *arrision* never caught on. Perhaps because it rhymes with *derision*.

## Aspectabund (adj.) *Having an expressive face.*

*Aspectabund* appears to be a word whose time has come and gone, its only citation in the *OED* being from the year 1708. As a word it is almost entirely forgotten; and perhaps soon, as cosmetic procedures continue to work their magic, the very notion of having an expressive face will be forgotten as well.

## Assy (adj.) *"Asinine."* (OED)

It is infinitely comforting to find that within the hallowed pages of this monumental work of scholarship, some lexicographer saw fit to insert at least one truly memorable four-letter word.

## Astorgy (n.) *A lack of natural affection.*

*Astorgy* seems to refer to the absence of love or affection toward the people in your life whom you should feel kindly toward— parents, children, and the like. It should not be taken as a substitute for the vague misanthropy that so many of us feel.
*also see:* unlove

## Atechny (n.) *A lack of skill; a lack of knowledge of art.*

Reading through the dictionary, I am struck again and again by the fact that many words that describe common things are obscure, while many words that describe obscure things are widely known. For example, everyone knows the word *dinosaur*, even though no one has ever seen or met one. Yet, even though we are faced each and every day with artistic ignorance and lack of skill, very few of us know the word *atechny*.

*also see:* cacotechny, mataeotechny

### Atrate *(n.) One dressed in black; a mourner.*

Although *atrate* is used rather specifically to describe a mourner, it is still quite nice to know that since at least the early seventeenth century there has been a word for that thoroughly modern character, the Goth teen (or average New Yorker) dressed all in black. We also have a word for describing someone who is wearing scarlet (*coccinated*) and the state of being dressed in purple (*porporate*).

### Avidulous *(adj.) "Somewhat greedy." (Nathan Bailey,* Dictionarium Brittanicum, *1731)*

Not excessively greedy, just somewhat greedy. The perfect word to describe such occurrences as when the cashier gives too much change and we neglect to draw his attention to it. The *OED* does not define it as such, but I like to think of *avidulous* as "acceptably greedy."

THE HEADACHES CONTINUE AS I READ, but they are not as troubling as they were when I was reading through *A*. It is not that they are any less severe, but I have come to view them in a different light. Whereas I previously looked upon them as an affliction, albeit a minor one, I now see them as a sign of progress. The more I read, the worse the headache will be. When I find a word that is particularly interesting my pulse will race just a little, and the headache will keep pace with my pulse, a more palpable indication of interest and excitement than a slightly increased heartbeat.

I've moved from merely being inured to these headaches to actively embracing them, and they in turn have taken on a life of their own. They keep their own schedule, one that more or less mirrors mine, although I think that they are lazier than I am. The first echoes of that delicious pang usually do not arrive until eleven in the morning, when I've already been reading for hours.

---

But the headache rolls up its sleeves and gets to work soon enough, and by the time lunch rolls around it seems to be considerably more energetic than I am.

It will usually proceed to keep its throbbing pace constant for the remainder of the afternoon, relinquishing its grip only several hours after I have stopped reading. On Saturdays, when I do not read the dictionary, I cannot help but feel something is missing from my body.

Perhaps it is absurd to attempt to measure how much work I've done based on the level of physical discomfort I feel. But when I've spent the past four hours sitting in a chair, buried in a book, and I finally stand up and find that my back cracks and my head pounds and the room spins a bit, well, it's depressing to simply think "I'm getting old, sitting here while I read this book," and so I choose instead to view the headache as a sign of accomplishment. I suppose I could take an aspirin, or do some exercises that are un-proven to relieve such pains, or even read less, but all of these op-tions seem uninviting.

The notes I've been keeping as I read have been giving me a headache of an entirely metaphorical nature as they become in-creasingly disorganized and incoherent. I am only partly through *B* and my apartment is becoming covered with bits and pieces of paper, splattered with words and ink blots. I have pieces of paper taped to the walls, lying on the floor, and inserted in the dictionary as bookmarks. I have come up with a system of abbreviations to write in the margins that tell me what is interesting about the words I've written down, and what else I want to find out about them. This system sometimes works quite well, and other times serves only to confuse me further. Recently I found a receipt on which I had written "! → ???*—Eutrapely—(more, & Shipley?)." I have no idea what this means.

After spending a number of hours trying to pull together all the scraps of paper, I decide I need a new system of keeping notes. I seek out and buy a ledger from the nineteenth century that has somehow managed to make it through more than a hundred years without anyone writing in it. It is a good-sized book, measuring fifteen by ten inches and weighing about six pounds, with five hundred pages of nicely yellowed paper.

It is large enough that I'll be able to fit all of my notes in it, and it makes for a pleasant and comforting weight as it sits on my lap. The more I read the more it becomes filled with a combination of jottings and coffee stains, testament to both my need for coffee and my inability to balance my cup on the book as I write.

Beethoven spent an enormous amount of time copying by hand the music of Bach and other composers he admired, as a means of learning their music. I have seen no evidence, nor do I expect to, that copying thousands of words and definitions will turn me into the lexicographic equivalent of a great German composer. But writing these words by hand, and letting the ink bleed into my fingers, is so far the only way that I've found of retaining them.

I balance the book and the coffee cup as I sit by the window in a large armchair, with my feet resting on an ottoman. On a small table to my right I keep extra papers, pens, and empty coffee cups.

To my left is the window, curtains drawn back, in case I want to look out at the street. I rarely do—if I glance up from the book it is usually to look across the room to where the bookshelves are.

A wall of dictionaries stands there, housed in a sturdy lattice of shelves that are painted a deep shade of red and extend from one side of the room to the other, from the floor to the ceiling. I built them some years ago, after discovering that the weight of my dictionaries was causing my store-bought shelves to fall apart. I'd wanted to get a rolling library ladder to go with them, but those are unreasonably expensive, so I instead built them with extra-thick wood so I can climb them like a ladder when I need to reach a book near the top. Most of the dictionaries on that wall exist in bits and pieces in the *OED*, and whenever I come across a citation from one I find that my eyes will dart over to the shelf where that book is housed.

I find *B* wildly entertaining. It's possible that I feel this way simply because of the enormous number of words that begin with *be-*, a sort of superprefix descended from Old English which has the power to form intensive and derivative verbs, turn substantives and adjectives into verbs, and do your laundry for you in its spare time. Stretching on for hundreds of pages, *be-* is responsible for such gems of the language as *bedinner* (to take to a dinner), *bespew* (to vomit on), and *bemissionary* (to annoy with missionaries).

*B* is also the letter in which I realize fully just how repetitious our language can be. A large number of words are more or less defined as "a stupid person," and even more words refer to a woman of dubious moral fiber (usually defined as "an untidy woman," a turn of phrase I believe had more pejorative connotations 150 years ago than it does today). Initially I wrote all these words down, fascinated that there should be enough interest in these things to warrant such a profusion of synonyms.

But as time wore on I realized that words to describe stupid people are not much more interesting than stupid people themselves. And while it is interesting that our language has such a variety of ways to describe untidy women, it does not interest me enough that I want to know what all of these words are.

Even though I do not feel a need to remember these words, I do feel a need to know that someone has remembered them. It is comforting to me to know that they have not been wholly cast aside, and are still available to anyone who cares to visit the *OED*, whether it is some poet trying to find the right word to make verse properly obscure or a head-scratching child trying to make sense of some obscure poet she's been assigned to read in school. The fact that the *OED* cares so much about words that almost everyone else happily ignores is one of its finest traits.

### Backfriend (*n.*) *A fake friend; a secret enemy.*

*Backfriend* is both useful and interesting, as we all seem to have friends who sometimes work against us. By no means is this the only word or phrase in the *OED* describing the type of friend who makes enemies seem more appealing. We also find:

> Fawnguest—*a person who pretends to be a friend in order to steal.*

Hindermate—*a companion who hinders more than helps.*
Job's comforter—*someone who pretends to be a comfort,*
*but who intends to cause distress.*
Night-worm—*a treacherous companion.*
*also see:* well-woulder

## Balaamite (*n.*) *One who is religious for the sake of monetary gain.*

According to the book of Numbers in the Old Testament, Balaam was a prophet whom the king of Moab directed to go meet with the Israelites so that he might place a curse on them. When he arrived at the Israeli encampment, however, Balaam refused to do so, on the grounds that Yahweh commanded him not to. A moving story, but unfortunately, somewhere after, in the neighborhood of 2 Peter 2:15, the story gets revised, and Balaam ends up being portrayed as a plain greedy bastard.

## Balter (*v.*) *To dance clumsily.*

It's nice to find a word I can use to explain why I've always hated to dance. I'm a balterer.

## Barla-fumble (*n.*) *In sport or play, a call for a pause or truce, from one who has fallen or is at a disadvantage.*

Every generation seems to have its own schoolyard version of what one cries out when seeking a truce. My friends and I would say "time out," and I've heard many other expressions such as "uncle," "I give," and so forth. It's ignominious enough to have to admit defeat without having to use a word that sounds as foolish as *barla-fumble*.

*also see:* superchery

## Bayard (*n.*) *A person armed with the self-confidence of ignorance.*

The word *bayard*, in its oldest sense, referred to a bay-colored horse. Unfortunately, the etymology of this word is largely unknown, so the path the word traveled to get from "horse" to "horse's ass" has been lost to us.

*also see:* ignotism

## Beadledom (*n.*) *The sense of self-importance and officiousness seen as characteristic of beadles, or minor officials.*

A beadle was a town crier, or one who made proclamations, a job that seems to have gone the way of the dodo. Stupid officiousness on the part of public officials, however, remains alive and well.

## Bedinner (*v.*) *To treat to dinner.*

So many other verbs that begin with this prefix appear to entail the act of throwing or projecting something unpleasant upon someone. For instance, *bespawl* is to splatter with saliva, *bescumber* is to splatter with dung, and *bevomit* . . . you can figure that one out on your own. It's pleasing to discover that *bedinner*, in contrast, does not connote a food fight.

*also see:* deipnosophist

## Bed-swerver (*n.*) *An unfaithful spouse.*

*Bed-swerver* sounds to me like a possibly gentler or more easily forgiven type of adultery, almost a euphemism, like "straying." After all, when one swerves, one can swerve back again.

## Bemissionary (*v.*) *To annoy with missionaries.*

This would be a delightful and whimsical word were it not for the fact that missionaries tend to be so irritating.

## Benedicence (*n.*) *Benevolence in speech.*

I suppose it makes sense that common occurrences should have more words to describe them, and less frequent occurrences should have fewer. Which would explain why the *OED* includes dozens of words that describe rudeness and ill will, whereas this is the only word I can remember finding that means kind conversation.

## Benignant (*adj.*) *Showing or having warm feelings toward one's inferiors.*

Further to the point above, how telling that *malignant* should survive, even flourish, while *benignant* has all but died out. The *OED* does mention in its definition that *benignant* has a suggestion of condescension to it.

## Bouffage (*n.*) *An enjoyable or satisfying meal.*

*Bouffage* comes from an Old French word of the same spelling, and in the etymology we find that Randle Cotgrave defined it in his 1611 French-English dictionary as "cheeke-puffing meat." Cheek-puffing just does not have the same currency as an indicator of satisfaction that it used to.

*also see:* gramaungere, moreish, quaresimal

## Bowelless *(adj.) Having no bowels; lacking in mercy or compassion.*

It was certainly news to me that having bowels was once a synonym for having compassion or pity. However, it existed not only with *bowelless*, meaning "having no pity," but also in such archaic phrases as *bowels of compassion* and *bowels of mercies*. I have decided that this is one of those word mysteries I would rather not delve into.

*also see:* immiserable

## Bully-scribbler *(n.) A bullying writer.*

It is difficult for me to take the notion of a bullying writer too seriously. Perhaps once upon a time this was a fearsome thought, but there is a good reason why today people think of the oafish thug in the schoolyard when they think of a bully—a punch to the jaw hurts more than an unflattering squib.

*also see:* anonymuncule

# C

To simply describe the *OED* as "large" is akin to saying that the bubonic plague was "unpleasant." It has 21,730 pages. Fifty-nine million words, give or take a few thousand. The most recent print edition, published in 1989, runs to twenty volumes and weighs exactly 137.72 pounds. It defines many hundreds of thousands of words and illustrates those words with almost two and a half million quotations. But it is not special simply because it is so large.

What is it that makes the *OED* special? The *OED* was not the first large multivolume work to be released: the seven-volume *Encyclopaedic Dictionary* of Robert Hunter was published in 1879, five years before the first fascicle of the *OED*. Neither was the *OED* the first large and multivolume English dictionary to be completed: the six-volume *Century Dictionary and Cyclopedia*, edited by Dwight Whitney, was finished in 1891 and subsequently rereleased in sets of five, eight, ten, and twelve volumes.

When it was first completed, in 1928, the *OED* didn't even have the most headwords of any dictionary. Various editions of *Funk and Wagnalls*, the *Century*, and *Merriam-Webster's* all claimed more headwords.

It was not the first dictionary to include citations from literature to show how words were used. Thomas Blount began doing that in 1656; Samuel Johnson did it a bit more enthusiastically in 1755; and from 1836 to 1838 Charles Richardson wrote an entire two-volume dictionary using only quotations, and no definitions, to illustrate the meanings of words.

So what exactly does it do that is so different?

Bigger does not necessarily mean better, except that the *OED* was designed to be bigger in ways that are better. One of the goals of the *OED* was, and still is, to trace the roots of each English word as far back as possible—not merely saying that a word entered the language in 1620 or 1750 and leaving it at that. The editors have spent an unknowable amount of time searching for the point at which a word (or a usage of a word) first entered the language, and they have also enlisted the services of an army of volunteer readers—thousands—to assist in this task.

If it didn't have more headwords than some other dictionaries at the time (it does now), how did the *OED* get to be so much bigger than the other dictionaries? Primarily through its citations of quotations to illustrate usage. The makers of the *OED* did not consider it enough simply to show how a word may have been used at some point in the past several hundred years; they wanted to show

# C

how it has been used at all points. Thus, a word that has been a part of the English language for the past eight hundred years will have myriad citations to show how it has changed in use as the language has also changed.

It is resolutely, obstinately, and unapologetically exhaustive. These qualities make it both a tremendous joy to read at some times and unbearably boring at others. I never have to worry that the *OED* has left out some crucial information about a word because the editors were trying to save space. True, the delegates from Oxford University Press who funded and published the *OED* did try their best to get the size winnowed down. But to give an idea of how expansive and learned this work is: at one point in the late nineteenth century, the delegates were demanding that the average entry in the *OED* be no more than *eight times* as long as the corresponding entry in *Webster's Third*.

It seems to me that the *OED* frequently assumes a certain level of scholarship in its readers—a level of scholarship that is not as common today as it was when the *OED* was first being written. For instance, the etymologies of words that come from ancient Greek are written in Greek. I do not find this terribly helpful, as I do not read Greek, ancient or modern. Under the entry for *syllogism*, the *OED* gives a nice, detailed definition and then proceeds to give an example of a syllogism. Which would be illuminating if not for the fact that the entire example is in Latin.

There are no pictures in the *OED*. Almost every other major dictionary of the past one hundred years has included illustrations.

As the marketplace for reference books became more competitive, dictionary makers fell into the habit of becoming more and more encyclopedic, including information such as pictures of all the state flags, color charts, and anatomical drawings. Even *Webster's Third* (which when published in 1961 was widely criticized for, among other things, moving away from encyclopedic information) has a full-page color plate with drawings of cats, and many other illustrations as well.

I do not mind the etymologies in Greek, and I do not mind having to dig out my old Latin dictionary from time to time. I certainly do not mind the absence of pictures, which I have always thought superfluous in books about words. Given how hard the compilers of the *OED* worked to bring it to fruition, it seems unfair to object to putting in a little work to read it.

## Cachinnator *(n.) A person who laughs too loud or too much.*

It struck me, as I read the definition of this word, that the cachinnator is a creature more common in our imagination than in real life. There really are not a great number of these vile people among us, and for a very good reason—I believe they are all killed by their parents at an early age.

*also see:* agelastic, hypergelast

## Cacotechny *(n.) "Bad art; a hurtful or mischievous art."* (OED)

Although both the etymology and the citations for this word

would seem to suggest that the art referred to is of the mechanical rather than the cultural sort, I cannot resist the temptation to take this word literally, since, as any moviegoer, theater fan, or gallery trawler will attest, there is such a glorious profusion of bad art of all kinds.

*also see:* atechny, mataeotechny

## Cacozealous (*adj.*) *"Ill-affected, or badly imitating."* (*Edward Phillips,* The New World of English Words, *1676*)

It is somewhat humorous that the definition of "badly imitating" supplied by the *OED* is taken directly from Edward Phillips's dictionary of 1676, given that Phillips himself blatantly imitated (some scholars say stole) the work of other lexicographers before him.

## Callisthenical (*adj.*) *Addicted to exercise or calisthenics.*

The pleasant thing about people who are *callisthenical* is that they generally wear themselves out and expire at an early age, sparing the rest of us the monotony of watching them, forever cheerful and virtuous, as they go about proudly proclaiming their bodies their temples.

## Cellarhood (*n.*) *The state of being a cellar.*

Along with *tableity* (the condition of being a table) and *paneity* (the state of being bread), *cellarhood* is a wonderful example of the spectacular ways English has of describing things that no ever thinks it necessary to describe.

**Charientism** (*n.*) *A rhetorical term to describe saying a disagreeable thing in an agreeable way.*

> If I knew how to say disagreeable things in an agreeable fashion I most likely would not be spending most of my time sitting alone in a room, reading the dictionary. I would have a real job that paid real money, perhaps something that involved glad-handing clients or some such nonsense.
>
> *also see:* garbist

**Chrestomathic** (*adj.*) *"Devoted to the learning of useful matters."* (OED)

> Although at first glance I thought this would be a terribly useful word, I soon discovered I couldn't find anyone who agreed on the definition of "useful matters." To some it's how to start a fire in the wilderness and to others it's how to get a bloodstain out of corduroy.
>
> *also see:* mataeotechny

**Cimicine** (*adj.*) *Smelling like bugs.*

> Growing up in a tenement in New York City, I had repeated exposure only to cockroaches, but since they move quickly I wasn't able to smell them up close. Also, I rather doubt that they had any more desire to be smelled by me than I had to do the smelling.

# C

---

**Coenaculous** *(adj.) Supper-eating, or, as the* OED *phrases it,* *"Supper-loving."*

Every once in a great while, a definition provided by the *OED* is startlingly conversational, as if someone at Oxford had declared they would have "casual-definition Friday," and the result was that the editors all let their hair down and came up with definitions like "supper-loving."

*also see:* bedinner, residentarian

**Colloquialist** *(n.) An excellent talker; a person who is good at conversing.*

*Colloquial* has long been one of the most misunderstood usage labels in dictionaries. From the Latin word *colloquium* (conversation), it has always been employed to refer to words as they are used in a conversational sense. However, so many people are under the impression that it means "slang" or "substandard" that some dictionaries have opted to stop using it.

*also see:* deipnosophist, eutrapely

**Compotation** *(n.) An episode of drinking or carousing together.*

*Compotation* is like the less successful younger brother of *symposium*. Both words originally meant nothing more than "a drinking party." But where *compotation* has apparently never sought to better itself, *symposium* has gone on to get its act together and add all sorts of other meanings to its résumé, such as "a meeting or conference," or "a book or essays on a subject."

---

## Conjubilant *(adj.) Being jubilant or rejoicing with another person.*

This may look like an odd word, and may even seem like an odd concept, were it not for the fact that were there a word for "rejoicing all alone, because there is no one who will share in your happiness," that would be even odder.

*also see:* letabund

## Conjugalism *(n.) The art of making a good marriage.*

Judging by the citation provided, from an 1823 article in *New Monthly Magazine* on the subject, magazines have been promising to teach us this particular secret for almost two hundred years now, and we still have not yet mastered it.

*also see:* levament

## Consenescence *(n.) "Growing old together; general decay."* (OED)

Perhaps it was unintentional, but it is nonetheless humorous that the *OED*'s editors saw fit to include the notions of decaying and growing old together in the same entry.

## Conspue *(v.) To spit on someone or something with contempt.*

I have not yet found any word that defines the action of spitting on someone or something for a reason other than contempt (can you spit on someone out of friendship or admiration?), and I have a strong suspicion that I will not. One who *conspues* is referred to as a *consputator*.

# C

### Constult (*v.*) *To act stupidly together.*

Taking part in an activity that is inordinately stupid just because one's friends are doing it is not the exclusive province of teenagers—it just seems that way.

*also see:* unasinous

### Countercozen (*v.*) *To cheat in return.*

In a curious moral twist, many people seem to feel that it is perfectly acceptable to cheat someone if he or she tried to cheat you first. Bearing this in mind, we can then look at countercozening as "justifiable cheating." At least some of us can.

*also see:* anti-rumour

### Credenda (*n., pl.*) *Things to be believed; articles of faith.*

*Credenda* are opposed to agenda, which are things to be done. I wonder if perhaps at some point in the less secular past people carried around twin sets of lists with them, agenda and credenda, so that they'd remember not just what to do for the day, but also what to believe in while they were doing it.

### Curtain-lecture (*n.*) *"A reproof given by a wife to her husband in bed." (Samuel Johnson,* A Dictionary of the English Language, *1755)*

It seems bizarre that a word with such a timeless quality to it (scolding one's husband) should be based on a practice (hanging curtains around the bed) that ended so long ago.

# D

I FULLY REALIZE I HAVE NO ONE but myself to blame for being in this position. No one ever approached me and said, "Mr. Shea, how would you like to spend the year confined to an armchair, reading the *OED*?" It was entirely my idea, and I do not try to blame anyone else for it. Well, except Madeline.

As far as I am aware, my friend Madeline is the only person in the world who ever made her living solely from buying and selling dictionaries. She is semiretired now, but was a full-time bookseller in this peculiar vein for several decades, and in the process she managed to amass a collection of dictionaries and a body of knowledge that are both fairly staggering. When people come by my house for the first time and express surprise or apprehension at the fact that I have a thousand or so books about words lying about I'll offer up Madeline as a way of explaining that my collection is actually rather small and manageable. She has at least twenty times as many as I do.

I met her eight years ago, after she read a book I had written about obscure words and sent me a letter, saying that she reasoned that I must be interested in dictionaries, and asking if I would perhaps like to pay her a visit to look at her collection. I went down to where she lives, in an elegant loft in lower Manhattan, and although I do not remember what I was expecting, I do remember that as soon as I entered her apartment I realized that whatever I had been expecting, it wasn't this.

There are only a few moments in my life when I have been literally struck speechless. Once was last year, when I ran a red light on my bicycle and a car traveling at thirty-five miles an hour ran directly into me, throwing me sixty feet through the air. When I stood up and discovered that I'd suffered nothing worse than a few scuffs I was so happy and surprised that I couldn't think of a single thing to say. Then I began laughing.

Another time was when I was eighteen years old, and had gone to Paris, the first time in my life I'd left North America. I was wandering around the city aimlessly and I happened into the cathedral of Notre Dame. The crowds of tourists around me were forgotten as I gazed up at its interior and tried to reason how and why such a ridiculous piece of splendor had ever come to be built. I was dumbstruck, and then after a few moments I began laughing.

So it was as I entered Madeline's apartment—she met me at the door, introduced herself and shook my hand, and then allowed me to walk in ahead of her. I made it through a short hallway choked with boxes and then walked into an enormous room with more dictionaries than I thought possible. Once again I was speechless, and then I laughed.

I stood there in the center of her living room and turned slowly in a circle, initially taking in just the quantity of books and after a few minutes beginning to take in their quality as well.

There were bookshelves, ten feet tall, on almost every wall in the room, with rolling ladders on runners. The rolling ladders looked as though they were not particularly functional, as additional piles of dictionaries, several feet tall and deep, had managed to accumulate on the floor in front of the shelves. Dictionaries lay on every possible surface—on tables, chairs, bookstands, the kitchen counter, and the floor. On the few spots of wall not taken up with dictionaries hung portraits of dictionary makers and framed letters to and from lexicographers both famous and forgotten.

One small shelf held nothing but dozens of miniature dictionaries, some the size of postage stamps. Nearby several rows of a bookcase were filled with enormous and antiquated books, dictionaries that would obviously require two hands and a strong back to read. A whole wall on one side of the room held dictionaries and other books on slang. Filing cabinets were stuffed with neatly arranged folders full of advertisements for dictionaries, reviews of dictionaries, and papers about dictionaries.

Madeline stood there and enjoyed my reaction for a few minutes more, and then gave me a tour of the books. And even though we never left the confines of this twenty-by-thirty-foot room it was still in its own way an exhausting tour. Over the next five hours we walked from the fifteenth century to the present, from Australia to New York, and from Samuel Johnson to Walt Frazier Jr. (the former New York Knicks basketball player and author of *Word Jam: A Guide to Amazing Vocabulary*).

It was immediately apparent that she knew where every one of the twenty thousand books in the apartment was. Furthermore, she could offer a witty and entertaining lecture on who had worked on any given book and what its lexicographical significance was and suggest other books that may have been influenced by it, all while balancing herself precariously on a ladder and tugging the book out from the shelves.

Madeline herself is somewhat diminutive and has a bushel of crinkly hair and perpetually twinkling eyes that suggest she is aware that she owns a collection that is miraculous to some small portion of the population, but not terribly exciting to the rest.

I had been collecting dictionaries in a somewhat desultory fashion prior to meeting her, picking up whatever odd volumes I found in thrift shops or the secondhand bookstores I frequented. This changed as soon as I met Madeline, and one of the first things I learned from her was that it was dangerous to go by to see her with money in my pocket. I'd tell myself that I was just going to stop in to say hello and have a quick visit, and that under no circumstances would I buy any more dictionaries. Then Madeline would show me some interesting book she'd lately come across, and casually mention that now she had this copy she might be able to sell me her old copy, and her price would always be so reasonable, and she always managed to make the books sound so fascinating, that I would inevitably wind up walking out of her apartment hours later, arms laden with several bags of books and my wallet considerably lighter.

No matter what sum of money I spent, I always left there with the firm impression that I'd got a bargain. The amount of information about dictionaries I've learned from Madeline is incalculable. Whenever I go to see her I make a list of all the things I want to ask her about beforehand, but we never make it to the end of that list. She has the habit of answering a question about one dictionary by pulling out a dozen others, and somehow makes the answers to my initial questions so entertaining that I forget what my other questions are.

I suppose that I would have continued to collect dictionaries even if I had not met Madeline. I would have shopped for the odd item here and there in bookstores, but they don't often get good dictionaries. And I'm sure that from time to time I would buy some overpriced book sight unseen on the Internet from a bookseller with whom I would have no contact at all, which is really not a satisfying way to shop for books.

However, I don't think I would have gotten ensnared in quite the same way had I not met Madeline. I didn't merely learn from her about words and their catalogers; I learned as well about the ineffable joy that can be had in pursuing the absurd. And there is something truly marvelous about such a fervid pursuit of something as absurd as collecting twenty thousand copies of what is essentially the same type of book, and it is endlessly inviting to see that someone who is so fascinating is engaged in it.

It is a certainty to me that without Madeline's influence and example I never would have been moved to read the *OED* from cover to cover. So I will say that I blame her for the position that I now find myself in, but what I mean by blame is that I credit her for helping me find happiness in the pages of one gigantic book.

### Dapocaginous (*adj.*) *Having a narrow heart.*

A somewhat literary insult rather than a medical term, *dapocaginous* goes nicely with *pusillanimous* (which comes from the Latin words for "narrow" and "soul").

### Debag (*v.*) *To strip the pants from a person, either as a punishment or as a joke.*

Oh, what a merry time it used to be, back in the days when it was still considered fun and games to rip the trousers from a person as a practical joke. Unfortunately, *debag* is a fairly recent word (the citations are all from the early- to mid-twentieth century) and it still appears to be a practice people engage in.
*also see:* sansculottic

### Deipnosophist (*n.*) *A person who is learned in the art of dining.*

Although I prefer the definition found in *Webster's Third* ("a person skilled in table talk"), the *OED* offers the bonus of another word, which most dictionaries do not have: *deipno-phobia* (fear of dinner parties).

*also see:* bedinner, colloquialist, eutrapely

## Desiderium *(n.) A yearning, specifically for a thing one once had, but has no more.*

*Desiderium* is the appropriate word for lost youth or innocence, for the great love of your life (who perished from consumption), or for the utopian community that you belonged to that was somehow destroyed by forces of evil. It is not the word for your lost wallet.

*also see:* remord

## Deteriorism *(n.) The attitude that things will usually get worse.*

The pessimist's nostalgia, *deteriorism* goes far beyond simply whining that things used to be better and takes the bold stance that the world is actively and energetically going to hell in a handbasket.

*also see:* pejorist

## Dilapidator *(n.) A person who neglects a building and allows it to deteriorate.*

The original meaning of *dilapidate* (from the Latin *dilapidare*, to squander) was to allow a building to fall into a state of disrepair. In New York dilapidators are simply known as landlords.

*also see:* grimthorpe

## Dis- *(prefix)*

To get from *disability* to *disyoke* in the *OED* takes 163 pages. Despite moments of mind-numbing tedium as one slogs through this distended corridor of entries, *dis-* is one of the most enjoyable prefixes in the alphabet. These pages have many words worth knowing, but I do not want to force too much of any one prefix down the throat of a reader. Here are just a few selections:

Disasinate—*to deprive of stupidity.*

Discalceate—*to take one's shoes off.*

Disconfide—*the opposite of* confide.

Discountenancer—*one who discourages with cold looks.*

Disfavourite—*a person who is the opposite of a favorite.*

Dispester—*to get rid of a nuisance.*

Dissight—*an unpleasant sight, an eyesore.*

Dissociety—*mutual dislike.*

## Dulcarnon *(n.) A person in a dilemma.*

The quotation the *OED* provides for *dulcarnon* is from Richard Stanyhurst's "A Treatise Contayning a Playne and Perfect Description of Irelande," published in 1577, which is a stern and eloquent account of some poor waverer's dilemma between choosing infidelity and the flames of hell on one hand or Christianity and the joys of heaven on the other. I myself will think of the word when choosing between such things as one lump of sugar or two, and imagine Stanyhurst rolling over in his grave.

**Dyspathy** *(n.)* *The antithesis of sympathy.*

I suppose that *antipathy*, a common enough word, fulfills much the same role, but I like the idea of a word whose sole meaning is "the opposite of sympathy."

# E

THERE HAS NOT BEEN A GREAT DICTIONARY written by a lexicographer working by himself since the early nineteenth century. It is just far too much work. The early dictionaries in English were frequently created by a single author, but they were small works, and not what we think of today as dictionaries. Robert Cawdrey's *A Table Alphabeticall*, published in 1604, is generally regarded as the first English dictionary. It was an impressive feat in many respects, but it contained fewer than 2,500 entries, the defining of which would not be a lifetime's work. This and the other dictionaries of the seventeenth century were mostly attempts to catalog and define "difficult words"; little or no attention was given to the nuts and bolts of the language or to such concerns as etymology and pronunciation.

For most of the seventeenth century dictionaries continued to be compiled by individuals, frequently at the behest of booksellers (who at that time acted much as publishers do today). Lexicographers cheerfully and blatantly stole from their predecessors, which I imagine relieved some of the drudgery and hard work of writing a dictionary. In 1658, Edward Phillips had the gall not only to plagiarize a great deal of Thomas Blount's dictionary of 1656, but to then accuse the man he had stolen from of inaccuracy and poor scholarship.

Samuel Johnson famously wrote his dictionary of 1755 by himself. Noah Webster worked largely unaided, on both his small compendious dictionary of 1806 and his much more impressive two-volume work of 1828. Charles Richardson likewise was the sole author of his two-volume work published in 1836 and 1837. Each of these dictionaries was innovative and singular in some way, and very different from the others, but they all have one element strongly in common: each is indelibly stamped with the personality of the man who wrote it.

Johnson's dictionary is probably as famous for the wit and bite of a number of the definitions as it is for its remarkable scholarship. Generations of individuals who would never think to look at his dictionary nonetheless know that he defined *oats* as a grain which "in England is generally given to horses, but in Scotland appears to support the people."

Webster was passionate about creating a separate American dictionary, with spellings and definitions of words that would be distinguished from those of British lexicographers. His 1828

E

dictionary is also so definitely marked by his religious beliefs that
a facsimile reprint of it is quite popular today with some Christian
groups, who approve of his biblically tinged definitions of such
words as *marriage*, *sin*, and *husband*.

Richardson's dictionary was . . . well, one cannot quite call it
famous; in fact, it is almost completely unknown outside of lexicographic circles. But within these circles it is quite well known, in
large part because of his decision to eschew definitions completely
and instead to illustrate the meanings of words through literary
quotations, which proved to be a significant influence on the *OED*.
Each of these three works is eminently recognizable as the creation of its author.

In contrast, the *OED* is not the creation of any one individual.
There have been a number of editors, and it is still very much a
work in progress, so there will doubtless be future editors who will
in turn leave their own personal imprint upon it. The original edition had four editors: James Murray as the editor in chief, Henry
Bradley, C. T. Onions, and W. A. Craigie. Robert Burchfield was
the editor for the four-volume supplement in the years between
1957 and 1986, and the current chief editor is John Simpson. One
could also count Herbert Coleridge, who was editor from 1859
to 1861, when he fell ill with tuberculosis and died. Although
Coleridge did not preside over any of the published work, he still
had a marked influence on it.

But even though a number of people influenced the *OED*, the
single most apparent presence is certainly that of James Murray.

Though the dictionary is not his creation alone, it has his personality writ large, both in the sections that he personally defined as well as those that he shaped merely through his suggestions. I may be confused sometimes about which of the other editors provided a definition or comment, but I feel I can always identify when it was Murray. His voice, always erudite, frequently cranky, and sometimes both, is almost immediately recognizable.

For instance, I know that Murray edited *P*, but even if I didn't, I think I could have guessed it. Under the entry for *pn-* is one of the rare editorial notes to appear in the *OED*. It contains Murray's reasons for why the *p* at the beginning of this prefix should be pronounced (chiefly, because all the other Europeans do so) and ends in a gently scolding tone: "the reduction of *pneo-* to *neo-*, *pneu-* to *new-*, and *pnyx* to *nix*, is a loss to etymology and intelligibility, and a weakening of the resources of the language."

Murray was on occasion wonderfully cantankerous, and not above nursing a grudge when he felt that either he or his dictionary had been slighted. In *Lost for Words: The Hidden History of the Oxford English Dictionary*, her marvelous book about the editing of the *OED*, Lynda Mugglestone recounts how Murray responded to the intemperate criticism of Benjamin Jowett, the head of Oxford University Press, who remonstrated Murray for what he perceived as an incorrect use of the word *due*. Murray said nothing at the time, but fourteen years later, when writing the entry for *due*, he inserted an example of Jowett using this word in the exact same way that he had previously criticized.

# E

Whenever I feel that I am on a fool's errand, and that my year might be spent in some more productive activity than this, I think of Murray, and the thirty-six years that he devoted to creating this dictionary. And then I realize that the reading I am engaged in is a privilege, not a task, and even if the dictionary were doubled in size I would want to read it still.

**-ee** (*suffix*) *One who is the recipient or beneficiary of a specific action or thing.*

With -*ee* attaching itself to so many interesting words, it seems rather a shame that the only ones still in common use today are pedestrian examples such as *employee*, *escapee*, and *divorcée*. In the interest of expanding your descriptive range I have included the following examples:

Affrontee—*a person who has been affronted.*

Beatee—*a person who has been beaten, as opposed to beater.*

Borrowee—*the person from whom a thing is borrowed.*

Boree—*one who is bored.*

Complainee—*a person who is complained about.*

Discontentee—*one who is discontent.*

Flingee—*a person at whom something is flung.*

Gazee—*a person who is stared at.*

Laughee—*someone who is laughed at.*

Objectee—*either a person who is objected against or a person who objects.*

Sornee—*one who has been sponged upon by others for free food or lodging.*

## Elozable (*adj.*) *Readily influenced by flattery.*

Given that just about everyone is capable of being flattered to some extent, I think this word should be reserved for those who are particularly amenable to it, such as writers of books about obscure words.

*also see:* expalpate

## Elucubration (*n.*) *Studying or writing by candlelight.*

From the Latin *elucubrare* (to compose by candlelight), *elucubration* is the word to describe staying up late while engaged in putatively productive endeavors, as opposed to just staying up late and watching TV.

## Elumbated (*adj.*) *"Weakened in the loins."* (OED)

A very delicate treatment of a possibly salacious word. The *OED* does not seem to specify what the cause of the weakening is, so use this word with care.

## Embusque (*n.*) *A person who avoids military service, especially through securing a job in government or the civil service.*

I presume that ever since there has been a military there have been people eager to avoid serving in it. While being an *embusque* (which with a touch of irony comes from the French word *embusquer*, to ambush) may not be the most honorable way of going about it, it certainly is more prudent than some others, such as shooting off a toe.

## Empleomania (*n.*) *A manic compulsion to hold public office.*

I would suggest that anyone who, in this day and age, is stricken with the urge to hold public office is deserving of this diagnosis, and should immediately be banned for life from "serving" the public in any capacity that requires more responsibility than that of a hot dog vendor.

## Enantiodromia (*n.*) *The adoption, by either a community or an individual, of beliefs opposite to those previously held.*

The word that describes what happened to your childhood friend who went from being a free-spirited and interesting person to getting his MBA, working at a stock brokerage firm, and living in a gated community. The word to describe the friend himself is *schmuck*.

*also see:* hansardize

## Engouement (*n.*) *Irrational fondness.*

It is not at all clear to me why a French word meaning "obstruction in the throat" would come to be used in either French or English to mean unreasoning fondness. Nonetheless, *engouement* has the potential to be a remarkably useful word, covering everything from someone who enjoys eating snails to someone who enjoys Jerry Lewis.

## Epizeuxis (*n.*) *The repetition of a word with vehemence and emphasis.*

As in "No, no, no!," "Yes, yes, yes!," or the ever popular "Why me? . . . Dear God, why me?"

## Essoiner (*n.*) *A person who offers an essoin, or an excuse for the absence of another.*

*Essoiner* is a legal term, and properly designates a person who is officially authorized to present an excuse. I would not mind having one myself, and I am certainly prepared to officially authorize anyone who would care to make excuses for me.

## Esurient (*adj.*) *Hungry, in a figurative sense; also, poor and greedy.*

The *OED* states that this word is now "humorously pedantic," a designation it frequently gives to absurd or ludicrous words. This always leaves me scratching my head, since while the words are very frequently pedantic, there is nothing at all humorous about this word, in either of its meanings.

## Eumorphous (*adj.*) *Well formed.*

I felt much the same way when I found this word as I do when I come across a physical object that is itself well formed, and it does not matter whether it is a building that is well built or a cup of coffee well brewed; I'm always pleased in a rather hard-to-define fashion.

## Eutrapely (n.) *Pleasantness in conversation.*

The *OED* contains no definition as such for this word; the editors instead rely on citations from earlier dictionaries. Most of these works seem to refer to *eutrapely* as "courtesy," but there is also a note that mentions the word was originally used by Aristotle to describe "pleasantness in conversation," a concept that has far fewer words to describe it than does courtesy, perhaps because it's such a rare quality.
*also see:* colloquialist, deipnosophist

## Exauspicate (v.) *To do something in an unlucky fashion.*

One of the many meanings of the word *auspicate* is "to give a fortunate beginning to." One of the many meanings of the prefix *ex-* is "to take away, or deprive of." Put them together and you get this Hindenburg of words.
*also see:* jettatore

## Excreable (adj.) *Being able to be spit out.*

This definition leads to the disturbing implication that there must also be things that cannot be spit out. I haven't yet come across the word for this yet, and rather fervently hope that I do not.

Exfamiliation *(n.) Exclusion from one's family.*

Just about every family has at least one member who has been excluded, either due to past actions or simply as a matter of principle, to keep the others on their best behavior.

*also see:* storge

Expalpate *(v.) To get something through flattery.*

*Toady, truckle, wheedle, cajole, fawn, blandish*—these are all perfectly fine words that have some meaning along the lines of "flatter." But unlike *expalpate*, none of them imply that one actually receives something from the flattery, making it all worthwhile.

*also see:* elozable

Exsibilation *(n.) The act of hissing someone off the stage.*

Whenever I hear or read of the grand old custom of hissing someone off the stage I think to myself, "Here is a thing that has been lost to our culture." In fact I mourn the loss of this far more than other departed social customs, such as rising from the table when a lady enters or exits, or teaching your child how to make seventeen different knots. This is the sort of knowledge we should be passing on to the next generation— how to hiss someone off the stage.

ONE OF THE QUESTIONS I HEAR most often regarding my plan to read the *OED* from cover to cover is "Why don't you just read it on the computer?" I usually respond as if the question was "Why don't you just slump yourself on the couch and watch TV for the year?" which is not quite an appropriate response. It is not so much that I am anticomputer; I am resolutely and stubbornly pro-book.

The *OED* was first released in computer format in 1989. While this initial attempt at a paperless dictionary was somewhat unwieldy to use, the newer electronic version is pretty spectacular. It can now be accessed online, which is how many people use it these days.

The electronic *OED* has an impressive arsenal of features, enabling its user to do things that are impossible to do merely by looking through the pages of a book. You can instantly find all the quotations by any cited author. You can find all the instances in which a specific word appears, and what's more, you can specify whether you want the computer to search for that word in the definitions, the etymologies, or anywhere else. If you misspell a word in the search box a very helpful sidebar lists the words that come before and after the nonexistent one you typed in.

With a click of the mouse you can view an attractive chronological graph of the history of a word's use. You can view all the latest entries that have been added to the dictionary or if you are feeling mildly antediluvian while in the midst of all this technology you can search through the older edition online. There is case-sensitive searching and exact character searching. There are filters for parts of speech and more options than I know what to do with. These are all wonderful functions; I have used all of them before, and will use all of them again.

But what about the things that you *cannot* do with the electronic version?

You cannot drop the computer on the floor in a fit of pique, or slam it shut. You cannot leave a bookmark with a note on it in a computer and then come upon it after several years and feel happy you've found something you thought you had lost. You cannot get any sort of tactile pleasure from rubbing the pages of a computer. (Maybe some people do get a tactile pleasure from rubbing their computers, but they are not people I have any interest in knowing anything about.)

Reading on a computer screen gives you no sense of time or investment. The page always looks the same, and everything is always in the same exact spot. When reading a book, no matter how large or small it is, a tension builds, concurrent with your progress through its pages. I get a nervous excitement as I see the number of pages that remain to be read draining inexorably from the right to the left. The fact that this will happen twenty times over as I read the *OED* does not in any way diminish its appeal.

I've never sat down at a new computer and, prior to using it, felt a deep and abiding need to open it up and sniff it as deeply as I can, the way I have with many a book. To me, computers all smell the same, and their smell is not a nice one. And though a computer will inarguably hold far more information than even the largest of books, sitting down at a computer has never provided me with that delicious anticipatory sense that I am about to be utterly and rhapsodically transported by the words within it.

I've never looked across the room at my computer and fondly remembered things that I once read in it. I can while away hours at a time just standing in front of my books and relive my favorite passages by merely gazing at their spines. I have never walked into a room full of computers, far from home, and immediately felt a warm familiarity come over me, the way I have with every library I've ever set foot in.

This is why I do not care to read the *OED* on the computer.

The copy of the *OED* I am currently reading is not even my favorite of the ones I own. The one I prefer to read is the 1933 edition, in its thirteen volumes of red buckram covers. The typeface is discernibly raised, and when I read it I keep my fingers splayed across its pages, enjoying the feel of the words on my fingertips.

I'm slightly abashed to admit that I own seven different copies of this dictionary. Aside from the twenty- and the thirteen-volume editions, I also have the four-volume supplement, both the two- and the ten-volume *Shorter Oxford English* dictionaries, the two-volume condensed type edition, and a random single-volume edition. Each of these works was created for a reason, and each has its own usefulness. It is only on rare occasions, such as when I'm moving, that I have any doubts as to whether I truly need them all.

Standing in front of the shelves in my living room and looking at all these variants of the same dictionary, representing as they do an impressive superfluity of information, it can be tempting to say that the computer renders them obsolete and unnecessary. But what does the computer know of the comforting weight of a book in one's lap? Or of the excitement that comes from finding a set of books, dusty and tucked away in the back corner of some store? The computer can only reproduce the information in a book, and never the joyful experience of reading it.

Faciendum *(n.) Something that should be done.*

Although judging by the quotations used, the true meaning of this word is somewhat close to "duty," I cannot help but think of it as referring to things that have to be done that I would rather not do, such as laundry and filing taxes.
*also see:* inadvertist

Fard *(v.) To paint the face with cosmetics, so as to hide blemishes.*

I suspect there is a reason no one ever gets up from the table and says, "Excuse me while I go to the ladies' room and fard." It seems to be very difficult to make a four-letter word that begins with *f* sound like an activity that is polite to discuss at the dinner table.

## Farouche *(adj.) "Sullen, shy, and repellent in manner."* (OED)

Not all people who are shy fall into the category of inoffensive wallflowers who are really quite delightful once you get to know them. Some people are shy because they've discovered that when they let their real personality shine through the world at large doesn't much care for them.

## Father-better *(adj.) Being better than one's father.*
## Father-waur *(adj.) Being worse than one's father.*

Both *father-better* and *father-waur* are Scottish terms, and it is interesting that they should distinguish being better than and worse than one's father, yet seemingly have no word for "being exactly as good as one's father."
*also see:* patrizate

## Fedity *(n., pl.) Vile or repulsive practices.*

It is never a bad idea to know one more word with which to describe foul or vile practices. Whether because you wish to condemn them or engage in them, it is certain to come in handy.
*also see:* insordescent

## Felicificability *(n.) Capacity for happiness.*

It seems rather a shame that such a beautiful concept should have such an unappealing and unwieldy word attached to it. Sometimes it is better not to create a word from a double handful of Latin roots, even if they were on sale at the time. Oh, well, you can't choose your parents.

*also see:* happify

## Filiism *(n.) An excessive bias for one's own son.*

It is surprising that *nepotism* (which comes from the Latin root for "nephew") should have pushed aside *filiism* (which comes, rather obviously, from the Latin root for "son"), but the ways of language, much like partiality for one's son, often make very little sense.

## Finifugal *(adj.) Shunning the end of anything.*

Many things in life deserve being finifugal about: the last twenty pages of a good book, a special meal that someone has just spent hours preparing for you, a slow walk in a light rain.

*also see:* indesinence

## Fleeten *(adj.) Having the color of skim milk.*

It is unclear to me why this is such a repulsive word. But it is.

## Fleshment *(n.) The sense of excitement that comes from an initial success.*

The sense of excitement that results from a first success can be a delightful thing to behold—witnessing the first time a child manages to ride a bicycle unaided, for instance. And for the person experiencing this *fleshment* (which, by the way, is a terrible-sounding word for such a potentially sweet concept), it can impart the feeling that anything in this world is indeed possible. Unfortunately, it can also have the same effect when you win some small amount of money the first time you play at craps—the mistaken illusion that the world is your oyster.

## Foiblesse *(n.) A distinctive weakness or a weakness for something.*

*Foible* has such an inelegant ring to it; it positively reeks of bad habits and decisions of dubious merit; in contrast, *foiblesse* makes the notion of having a weakness for something seem acceptable, even downright commendable.

*also see:* hamartia

## Fomes *(n.) "Any porous substance capable of absorbing and retaining contagious effluvia." (Robert Mayne,* A Medical Vocabulary, *1862)*

If you are one of those people who would rather balance precariously in the middle of a moving subway train rather than hold on to the same handholds as the rest of the disease-ridden public, or you're one of the contortionists who insists on opening bathroom doors with your elbow, this is the word for you. Pack it away in your brain, right next to the section that reminds you to buy more bleach and antibacterial hand wipes the next time you're at the drugstore.

*also see:* mysophobia

**Foreplead** *(v.)* *To ask too much in pleading.*

You are pleading when you ask for your job back; you are fore-pleading when you ask for a raise to go with it.

**Fornale** *(v.)* *To spend one's money before it has been earned.*

We live in a nation that is overwhelmingly and crushingly in debt, awash in credit card debt and subprime mortgages. How is it possible that the only word for "spending money before it is earned" is an obsolete Scottish one?

**Forplaint** *(adj.)* *Tired from complaining.*

It can indeed be tiring, having to constantly remind the world at large that it does not quite live up to your exacting standards. We should recognize those among us who are forplaint, and thank them for their selflessness in trying to better our world with their ceaseless haranguing and nitpicking.

**Frauendienst** *(n.)* *An exaggerated sense of chivalry toward women.*

An example of the evolving notion of chivalry. *Frauendienst* was the title of a thirteenth-century work by Ulrich von Lichtenstein, in which he details all the utterly remarkable things that he accomplished in the service of his preferred lady (defeating hundreds of opposing warriors, undergoing mutilation, and the like).

# G

WHEN I FIRST BEGAN READING THE *OED* I envisioned it as a project in which I would while away my days at home, flitting back and forth between a comfortable armchair and the kitchen, happily reading and occasionally staring ruminatively out the window. But it turns out that reading at home doesn't work very well. There are far too many distractions.

The car alarm that goes off every day at noon is a distraction. The neighbors upstairs, playing their horrible dance music and shuffling about in what sounds like metal-soled clogs, are a distraction. The couple across the hall who cook salt cod four days a week, opening the door to their apartment and ventilating the smell into mine, is a distraction. And most of all, having all my other dictionaries right here is a distraction.

I find myself constantly drawn to my bookshelves to check on something, whether it's a word that isn't in the *OED* but I think

I've seen somewhere else, years ago, or it's a definition I've just read in the *OED* that doesn't match what I think I've seen in some other edition of *Webster's Third* or *Funk and Wagnalls*. So I get up, telling myself that I'll just look for this one small thing, and the next thing I know I'm surrounded by competing dictionaries, all of which are clamoring for my attention. Thirty minutes run by, and while I may have leafed through twenty different definitions of some particular word, I haven't got any reading done.

So I decide to begin reading in libraries. You can find the *OED* in almost any major library, which is pleasant, as I do not enjoy lugging it around with me. It is like the Gideons Bible of the library system: ubiquitous, and yet I never see anyone using it. But someone must be reading it, as in each library I have visited the copy of the *OED* shows obvious signs of wear and use. Some are so heavily worn that I wonder if it is being used for some purpose other than as a reference book, as if someone has been stacking the volumes up and using them as a stepladder.

Each one has discernible signs of use, sometimes through a particular page being significantly grimier than the rest, and sometimes through impromptu editorializing. Entries will be crossed out, or exclamation points show up next to words that particularly interested someone. These words that have aroused the most interest usually seem to be ones with definitions someone might disagree with, such as epithets based on gender or race. Every single copy I have seen has had some pages ripped out, although it is not clear to me whether this happened because the reader was covetous of what was on the page and wanted to keep it, or was offended by it and wanted to keep it from the world.

Having many fond memories from my youth of the various New York City public libraries I decide they will be excellent places to read. I pack a bag with a lunch and some coffee and head down to the glorious main reading room of the Forty-second Street branch. My stay there lasts about three hours, enough time to be scolded by several clerks, to see at least three men who seem inordinately fond of scratching themselves, and to witness one fairly spectacular fistfight, complete with chairs and books being thrown and a phalanx of library guards charging into the room. This is all very entertaining, but not conducive to reading, so I set about finding another library.

I live near Columbia University, which has a total of nine different libraries, all of which are spectacular. You can purchase reading privileges for a fee, and while it may stick in my craw somewhat to pay for a library I have to admit it is well worth it. Unlike the public libraries, I've not once seen a fistfight at Columbia, and they generally do not have people using the bathroom sinks as showers. But their libraries are also fairly crowded, and have far too many interesting books, which is a constant source of distraction.

So I've ended up spending most of my time reading in the basement of the Hunter College library. The students here seem to be not as interested in studying as the ones at Columbia do, and many days I'm the only person in the basement. It is as quiet a spot as one can find in New York. I've dragged a desk over to a corner and sit with my back to the wall, looking out at a diminishing line of dozens of rows of bookshelves. I've chosen this corner because the books around me are all either about the theater or are written in French. I'm not interested in the theater and cannot read French, so I am able to sit here surrounded by the sight and scent of books without the danger of becoming unduly distracted by them.

Every morning I get up and make myself a cup of coffee. This coffee, once drunk, enlivens me enough to make more coffee, to consume throughout the day. I have an old Italian espresso press, one that requires a certain level of interaction to operate. To get the coffee out of the machine I have to pump the arm up and down a few times. It has numerous valves and gadgets on it that I don't quite understand. I don't need to understand how they work; it still makes a fine coffee.

I fill a thermos with espresso: fill it almost to spilling, until the oily surface of the black liquid peeks up near the rim. Every morning I tell myself that this quantity of espresso will last me throughout the day. It never lasts until noon. I chide myself gently for having drunk all my coffee so early in the day and then happily go out and buy more, filling my thermos again and descending back into the library. Coffee has long since transcended its role as "the thing that wakes me up" and is now comfortably settled in the role of "the thing that brings me joy." In some ways, it's also the thing that allows me to read the *OED* from cover to cover.

ALTHOUGH THERE ARE FAR FEWER distractions here than at home, it does not mean that this library is free of them. There is a certain type of person who seems to go to libraries expressly to talk, the conversational variant of nature abhorring a vacuum. I have turned into the ogre of the library basement, and have progressed from politely asking people to keep their voices down to energetically shushing as soon as they talk for more than a few minutes.

I did not plan on becoming a public shusher, at least not until I was considerably older than I am now. Lately I've been making an effort to restrain myself from engaging in this activity. But there have been occasions, such as when a bevy of drama students decided that my corner of the library was the perfect spot to practice dialogues, when I could not restrain myself. Their response to my yells of outrage ("We're sorry . . . we didn't know anyone would be *reading* here") instantly saddened me. First, because I had not needed to be as brusque as I'd been, and second, because they really could not comprehend that someone would be reading in a library.

Since then I've also tried to be more politic when asking people not to talk. And even when I feel that the talkers do not deserve politeness I no longer yell. Instead, I tell them that there are rats in this portion of the basement. I say that the only reason I mention this is that someone had a rat crawl into his bag just last week, and unwittingly took it home with him. Very few of them remain in the basement after that.

There are no rats in the library. There is only the occasional mouse, and the mice are unfailingly polite, and never raise their voices.

**Garbist** *(n.) One who is adept at engaging in polite behavior.*

I find that my view on what is polite behavior mirrors the view that former Supreme Court justice Potter Stewart had on pornography—I cannot define it but I know it when I see it. I am always pleased to make the acquaintance of a garbist, even though I'm not much of one myself.

*also see:* charientism

**Gastrophilanthropist** *(n.) "A benevolent purveyor for the appetites of others."* (OED)

When I first came across this word I was certain it was no more than a fancy nineteenth-century term for "pimp." But this is not the case, and it seems that once upon a time it was possible to use the words *purveyor*, *appetites*, and *others* all in conjunction and not mean anything dirty by it.

**Gaum** *(v.) To stare vapidly.*

Gauming is easily identified as the behavior of mouth-breathers and simpletons the world over, so be sure not to mistake it for *gaum-like*, which is defined as "having an intelligent look."

*also see:* gove

**Goat-drunk** *(adj.) Made lascivious by alcohol.*

According to the redoubtable Thomas Nashe, the author of *The Anatomie of Absurditie, Christ's Teares over Jerusalem*, and many other important works of English literature, there are eight types of drunkards, of which the one who is goat-drunk is seventh, although it is unclear what the order signi-fies. Since the *OED* has seen fit to include only a few from Nashe's list I have decided to include it in its entirety, so that you may never be at a loss for words when confronted by a drunk of any sort.

1. Ape-drunke—*"he leapes, and sings, and hollowes, and daunceth for the heavens."*

2. Lion-drunke—*"he flings the pots abut the house, calls his Hostesse whore, breakes the glasse windows with his dagger, and is apt to quarrell with any man that speaks to him."*

3. Swine-drunke—*"heauy lumpish, and sleepie, and cries for a little more drinke."*

4. Sheepe-drunke—*"wise in his owne conceipt, when he cannot bring forth a right word."*

5. Mawdlen-drunke—*"when a fellowe will weepe for kindnes in the midst of his Ale, and kisse you, saying; By God Captaine I loue thee, goe thy waies thou dost not thinke so often of me as I do of thee, I would (if it pleased GOD) I could not loue thee so well as I doo, and then he puts his finger in his eie, and cries."*

6. Martin-drunke—*"when a man is drunke and drinkes himselfe sober ere he stirre."*

7. Goat-drunk (*See above.*)

8. Foxe-drunke—*"when he is craftie drunke, as many of the Dutch men bee, and neuer bargain but when they are drunke."*

I knew I should never have bargained with that soused Dutchman.

## Gobemouche (*n.*) *One who believes anything, no matter how absurd.*

From the French words *gober* (to swallow) and *mouche* (fly).

*also see:* superfidel

## Gound (*n.*) *The gunk that collects in the corners of the eyes.*

*Gound* is the perfect example of a word that is practically useless, and yet still nice to know. It is the type of word I was unaware that I didn't know, and yet it still felt like a relief when I discovered it, as though I'd finally managed to remember that troublesome word I'd forgotten years ago.

## Gove (*v.*) *"To stare stupidly."* (OED)

Dictionaries are supposed to be objective records of our language. While not necessarily intended to be passionless, they have largely eschewed the role of being the arbiters of the language, instead choosing to record it as it is used by its speakers and writers. The great dictionaries of English have done a remarkably thorough job of living up to very exacting standards, not changing a word merely because they do not like it. And so, there is something interesting about the word *gove*. The *OED* defines it as "to stare stupidly." So do *Funk and Wagnalls*, the *Century Dictionary*, and the *Imperial Dictionary*.

In fact, every dictionary I have checked defines this word as "to stare stupidly" except for *Webster's Third New International*, which defines it as "to stare idly." I am quite sure that the fact that the editor of *Webster's Third* was named Gove had nothing to do with this decision.

*also see:* gaum

## Gramaungere *(n.) A superb or great meal.*

Although this is a fine-looking word with an amply interesting meaning and a good etymology (from the Old French *grant mangier*, great meal), the real enjoyment in reading it came from the rather inexplicable comment posted below the definition, which states: "not from the orig. Fr., which has 'do you think you can eat up all the pagans by yourselves?'" I'm not sure what original French they're referring to, but I wish they had included more of it.

*also see:* bouffage, moreish

## Grimthorpe *(v.) To restore or renovate an ancient building with excessive spending rather than with skill.*

*Grimthorpe* is a more or less eponymous word, taken from the title of Sir Edmund Beckett (the first Lord Grimthorpe), a lawyer and horologist in London, who also enjoyed attempting restorations of old buildings. His efforts did not meet with widespread approval, and gave birth to this word.

**Grinagog** (*n.*) *A person who is constantly grinning.*

Perhaps this should have also been defined as "one who deserves to be poked in the eye with a sharp stick."
*also see:* hypergelast

**Guestan** (*adj.*) *Appropriate for guests.*

The editors of the *OED* included a question mark before this entry, a habit they have when they are not entirely certain of the meaning. Which I think entirely fitting in this case, as this is a word that does and should mean different things to many people. To me, the notion of what is suitable for guests usually includes something to do with a locked door and unanswered doorbells.

**Gulchin** (*n.*) *A little glutton.*

The diminutive form of *gulch* (which presumably is a full-sized glutton).

**Gymnologize** (*v.*) *"To dispute naked, like an Indian philosopher."* (*Nathan Bailey,* An Universal Etymological English Dictionary, *1727*)

There are only several plausible reasons I can think of for having an argument while naked, and none of them happens to involve Indian philosophers.

I WORE GLASSES FOR MOST of my childhood, until I was nineteen and broke the only pair I owned. I couldn't afford to buy new glasses at the time and blurred through two months of severely impaired vision and friends thinking that I was ignoring them before my eyes somehow managed to strengthen themselves enough that I could see again. It is now almost twenty years later, and I have finally come to accept that my eyes, having loosened their grip on 20/20 vision, will not repeat that same trick of self-healing.

I have also come to accept that there is no way I will finish reading the *OED* without glasses, as every week I find that my nose is closer to the page, my eyes are more and more squinted, and my headaches are growing more and more insistent.

The optometrist I call on, after acknowledging the inevitable, is the same one that I went to twenty and thirty years ago, and the shop is comfortingly similar to how I remember it. It is located in the same small storefront and operated by the same mildly dour man, Myron. The only difference I can see is that the stools that used to be in front of the counter are gone. They were the same kind that one used to see at lunch counters, plain metal with colored vinyl seats. Upon entering the store my brother and I would immediately rush to sit on them and, kicking off from the counter, spin ourselves round until we became nauseated and dizzy. Myron says that he remembers me as one of the unpleasant children who helped break the stools before their time, and I doubt that he really remembers me, until it turns out that he also remembers what my last prescription was, from 1987.

If the storefront looks largely unchanged from my memories of twenty years ago, the small back room where the examinations are done looks like it is unchanged from the memories of someone much older than I. It smells like 1940, and most of the instruments look like they've been around for at least that long. There is an antique cabinet on one wall, filled with dozens of thin compartments, each holding a lens of a different strength, encased in black plastic. Underneath that cabinet I can see a dusty copy of *Gould's Medical Dictionary*, and I recognize it as being the same edition as the copy I have at home, which is from 1935.

I don't know why I find it reassuring to have medical equipment that is so out of date, but I do. I like the implied weight of the thing that swings out from the wall and functions as a giant set of testing eyeglasses, heavy metal encased in green enamel. I like the old cast-iron chair, which huffs and wheezes asthmatically as it is brought up and down to get my eyes at the correct height.

Myron clucks and fiddles with various lenses and asks me why I think I need glasses again. I explain, as briefly as possible, that I'm reading a large book, and it seems to be contributing to the accelerated decline of my eyesight. He clucks some more and clicks some dials, and asks me every few clicks whether I can now see the lettered chart better or worse than before. Ten minutes of this and we reach the unsurprising conclusion that I do in fact need glasses.

While Myron is writing the prescription I discover that glasses have become fashionable since last I wore them, and that, should I care to, I can spend more money on a small pair than I spent on the entire twenty volumes of the *OED*. I never quite trust objects that become more expensive as they become smaller, and I do not care to have six hundred dollars swimming out of my wallet to sit atop my nose. I buy one of the cheaper options, a clunky pair of tortoiseshell horn-rims, made in China and emblazoned with the word *gentleman* on the inside of one of the arms.

As I'm leaving I ask Myron if there is any advice he can give me that will make the task of reading small and uneven type for ten or twelve hours a day any easier. He raises his eyebrows and looks at me over the top of his own glasses (a habit that people who wear glasses use to indicate skepticism and sometimes contempt) and curtly says, "Yes—you could read less." With this established I decide that I will not ask Myron for any more advice.

When I get back to the library and resume reading I immediately realize why people wear these silly little things—they make your vision better. I no longer have to move my face closer to or farther from the page depending on whether I am reading the definition or the etymology. The headaches do not go away, but they become less severe. And at the end of the day I do not have large patches of gray imposing themselves on my peripheral vision. I am considerably cheered by this improvement, and wish that I could get glasses for all the other parts of my body that don't work as well as I would like them to.

## Halfpennyworth (*v.*) *To bicker over minute expenses.*

A word that nicely captures the pettiness of this habit.

## Hamartia (*n.*) *The flaw that precipitates the destruction of a tragic hero.*

*Hamartia* is a noble word, with a fine history (the *OED* says also that it refers particularly to Aristotle's *Poetics*). If you have any decency or soul, please do not use this word to refer to your own weakness for something such as chocolate.
*also see:* foiblesse

## Hansardize (*v.*) *To show that a person has previously espoused opinions differing from the ones he or she now holds.*

From the names of Luke Hansard and his son, Thomas, who for many years published the *Journal of the House of*

*Commons*, the official report of what had been said in that august body. The word was originally used to describe confronting a politician with written evidence of his flip-flopping, but think of how useful it would be to have a *hansardizer* around whenever you needed to remind someone in any walk of life that they have changed their opinions.

*also see:* enantiodromia

## Happify *(v.) To make happy.*

*Happify* appears to have been used as a verb for quite some time, ranging from the works of Josuah Sylvester in the early seventeenth century all the way up to Lou Shelly's *Hepcats Jive Talk Dictionary* of 1945. It has such a pleasing ring to it that I'm mystified that it has not been retained more in common usage.

*also see:* felicificability

## Heredipety *(n.) The hunting of an inheritance.*

Had this word existed in Shakespeare's time it might well have referred to such activity as killing off all one's brothers. Today it would likely be reduced to swiping the family silver before the rest of your siblings show up.

## Hetaerocracy *(n.) The rule of members of a college; the rule of courtesans.*

It is not often that the members of a college and courtesans are mentioned in the same sentence, much less defined in the same word, so perhaps a quick explanation is in order. Both senses of the word are based on the male and female forms of a Greek word; the male *hetairos* translates as "companion, fellow," and the female *hetaira* translates as "companion" as well, but with shades of meaning that vary from concubine to courtesan.

## Heterodogmatize *(v.)* *To have an opinion different from the one generally held.*

Just because you are in proud possession of opinions that differ from those of the majority of the population is no reason to start patting yourself on the back. Usually it just means you are wrong.

*also see:* homodoxian

## Heterogenic *(adj.)* *"Occurring in the wrong sex, as a beard upon a woman."* (*W. A. Newman Dorland,* The Illustrated Medical Dictionary, *1900*)

Almost every dictionary that I've seen illustrate this word uses the odd example of "like a beard on a woman." I am not one for railing against gender inequity in the dictionary, but this has always stuck in my craw. Large breasts on men are a far more common example of something occurring in the wrong sex than beards on women, but I've yet to see a single dictionary use this as an example.

## Heterophemize *(v.)* *To say something different from what you mean to say.*

Think back on all the things you've said in life that you truly wish you hadn't. Wouldn't it be nice if you could just claim afterward that you had been *heterophemizing*, and be instantly forgiven?

## Homodoxian (*n.*) *A person who has the same opinion as you.*

A very fancy word for "friend," "assistant," or "someone who's got their head on straight."
*also see:* heterodogmatize

## Hooverize (*v.*) *To be exceedingly sparing, especially with food.*

Poor Herbert Hoover. The thirty-first president of the United States not only presided over the country's descent into the Great Depression, he also found himself the eponymous root of two less than stellar words, *Hooverize* and *Hooverville*. Hoover was the United States Food Commissioner during the years 1917 to 1919, and his stewardship of that agency during and immediately after the war years led to charges that he was overly stingy with food rationing. He later was president of the United States at the beginning of the Great Depression and, whether fairly or not, became identified with the failure of government relief efforts. As a result, the shantytowns that were erected by hordes of indigents (*Hoovervilles*) came to be named after him as well.

## Horn-face (*n.*) *A stupid face, such as a cuckold might have.*

There exists a gross inequity between the sexes in terms of how many English words there are for a person who is unchaste (words for women outnumbering those for men by a great deal). This discrepancy extends itself as well to the number of words to describe a person whose spouse has been unfaithful, there being many more words and terms for men who have unfaithful wives. A partial list of terms for men who have been cheated on includes the words *actaeon, becco, half-moon, hoddy-poddy, summer-bird,* and *wittol.* Only one word is listed in the *OED* for a woman who has an unfaithful husband: *cuckquean.*

**Hot cockles** (*n.*) *"A rustic game in which one player lay face downwards, or knelt down with his eyes covered, and being struck on the back by the others in turn, guessed who struck him."* (OED)

When I first came across this game, which, judging from the quotations, was current from the late sixteenth through the early nineteenth centuries, I thought warm thoughts to myself about how far we have progressed as a society, that we no longer engage in such barbaric sport. Then I remembered the games of my childhood, not so long ago. Games such as Knuckles, which primarily consisted of removing the skin from the hand of an opponent using a deck of playing cards, and Dodgeball, using fireworks instead of a ball. Perhaps we have not progressed so far.

**Hypergelast** (*n.*) *A person who will not stop laughing.*

It's still up in the air whether the *hypergelast* or *agelastic* is more annoying.

# H

Cole Porter famously wrote in a song that all the world loves a clown, and it's true, the whole world indeed does. Except when the clown won't stop laughing, at which point the whole world decides it hates him. As well it should, because people who will not stop laughing are quite possibly the worst people of all.

*also see:* agelastic, grinagog

I FEEL AS THOUGH I AM EATING the alphabet. Twenty-six courses of letters, each with its own distinctive flavor. It is inevitable that some letters will taste delicious, others not so much. Some will have a delicate flavor, others will be more like a hearty peasant stew. Some will just taste unpleasant. The letter *I* tastes like it is full of capers, and I hate capers.

The caper in this instance is a peculiar little word formation, the *i-* prefix. It usually designates the past participle form of a word in Early Middle English, and apparently was quite the rage once upon a time, as the portion of the dictionary I am now reading is full of the damned things. These are sure signs that I am losing my mind—not only that I am attributing culinary characteristics to letters of the alphabet, but also that I am able to nurse a grudge against a prefix.

I am of course aware that these entries need to be in the *OED*, as they are a part of our language's heritage, and I am also aware of the fact that if I had not decided to read the dictionary I wouldn't have to wade through all these irritating past participles. But at this point I can't be bothered with such niceties as common sense—I'm just sick of reading words with a little *i-* in front of them: "i-lend is the pa. pple. of lend," and "i-called is the pa. pple. of call," and so on and so forth. It does not take many such entries for me to feel nauseated.

I realize that reading the dictionary is not all fun and games. That is not quite true, for me it is fun and games, but there are points at which I get bored, or irritated. There are also points at which I become utterly confused about why the dictionary is the way it is, and wish I had a lexicographer on standby to explain it to me.

As it turns out, I do have a lexicographer on hand, albeit a former one, in the form of my girlfriend. She knows far more about the nuts and bolts of the dictionary than I do. This is not surprising, as I only read them, and furthermore, I read them with the uncritical eye of a fan, and she has actually worked at writing them.

When Alix and I were first dating, I received an e-mail from her that made use of the word *catty-cornered*. Having just recently learned the etymology of this word (it comes, ultimately, from the French *quatre*), I wrote her back and casually made mention of this fact. Her response to this was to send me a several-page-long article that she'd written for Merriam-Webster on the subject. I couldn't remember ever being quite so embarrassed and exhilarated at once.

So when I come up against something like the proliferation of *i-* words in my epic reading project, my first impulse is to ask Alix about it. However, she is fiercely and unapologetically pro-Merriam-Webster. When I asked her thoughts as to why all these words were included in the *OED* and yet were not defined, she sniffed disdainfully, shook her head, and said, "Well, they've never really been much of a *defining* dictionary."

I have the feeling that this prejudice she has is not overtly anti-*OED*; she just doesn't understand why I, or anyone else, would choose to read a dictionary that was not published by Merriam-Webster.

## Iatrogenic *(adj.) Pertaining to symptoms caused unintentionally by a doctor.*

I cannot think of a single word that means "cured by a doctor." This is why I do not go to the doctor.

## Idiorepulsive *(adj.) Self-repelling.*

*Idiorepulsive* seems to be a word of scientific nature and use. However, since it is buried in the middle of a large pile of other *idio-* words, there is no way of knowing whether it has ever been used in a nonliteral sense. And I cannot think of any restrictions (aside from those that dictate good taste and proper use of language) that would prohibit me from using this in a strictly figurative sense, as a more emphatic means of describing self-hatred.

## Ignotism *(n.) A mistake made from ignorance.*

It is debatable whether an *ignotism* represents a more excusable form of error than one due to laziness or lack of care. I guess it depends on whether the error in question is on the order of someone giving wrong directions or a doctor removing the wrong limb during surgery.

*also see:* bayard

## Illutible *(adj.) Unable to be washed away.*

A word that suits a wide range of subjects, from bicycle grease to adultery.

*also see:* abluvion

## Ill-willy *(adj.) Cherishing malevolence.*

Not to be confused with *evil-willy* (which describes merely the possession of desires that are evil), *ill-willy* is a state of cherishing malignancy. And although the definition sounds as though it should be applied to some dramatic form of unpleasantness, it's hard to take any word that ends with *-willy* too seriously.

*also see:* stomaching

## Immiserable *(adj.) "Whom none pittieth." (Henry Cockeram, The English Dictionarie, 1623)*

From the Latin *immiserabilis* (unpitied). It should come as no surprise that this word comes to us from ancient Rome;

not only are most of the words in our vocabulary descended from Latin, the Romans raised the practice of not pitying to a high art.

*also see:* bowelless

## Immutual (*adj.*) *Not mutual.*

There is really no way that something *immutual* is pleasant. I've tried to think of an *immutual* circumstance I would like to find myself in and all I can think of is unrequited love and unwanted friendships.

## Impedimenta (*n., pl.*) *Such things as impede progress.*

Although *impedimenta* has most often been used in the sense of some concrete thing (such as baggage) that impedes progress, I prefer to think of it when I encounter any of the general things that slow one's progress through life, such as having a moral code of some sort.

## Impluvious (*adj.*) *"Wet with rain."* (*Thomas Blount, Glossographia, 1656*)

The *OED* does not provide any quotations for this word; it only mentions the fact that it existed in two dictionaries, hundreds of years ago. While I am not generally in favor of resuscitating a word that has died a natural death, I would make an exception in the case of *impluvious.*

*also see:* petrichor

**Inadvertist** *(n.) One who persistently fails to take notice of things.*

The *inadvertists* are those who stumble through life seemingly with no other purpose than to make it difficult for the rest of us—the ones who splay their legs wide on the subway, decide to get rid of all their small coins at the supermarket, and stand at the front of a long line at the airport asking about flights two months in advance.

*also see:* faciendum

**Incompetible** *(adj.) Not within the range of a person's competence.*

Sensing confusion in its reader, the *OED* cautions that this word is sometimes confused with *incompatible*, which has a slightly different meaning. *Incompatible* might describe the wrong tool for the job; *incompetible* describes the wrong person for it.

**Indesinence** *(n.) Want of proper ending.*

One of the things I find nice about reading the dictionary is that I always know what the ending will be, and I've yet to be unsatisfied with it. I believe this word is referring more to a sense of ending as in "never-ending" rather than "crap-Hollywood-movie type of ending," but it's not entirely clear.

*also see:* finifugal

## Indread (*v.*) *To feel a secret dread.*

We all have some nameless fear, a source of secret dread that keeps us awake at night from time to time, sickened with worry. Now you know what to call it, which will not in any way help in dispelling it.

*also see:* terriculament

## Indri (*n.*) *Babacoote.*

This word is included for the benefit of all those language purists who insist that English is a very pure and noble language and must not be tampered with in any way. *Indri* comes to our language from the French naturalist Sonnerat, and nicely illustrates the often inglorious fashion in which words are sometimes created. Sonnerat was in Madagascar around the year 1780, in search of the babacoote, a type of lemur that lives in trees. The word for this animal in Malagasy is *babakoto*; however, that is not the word Sonnerat came up with. He decided to name the animal *indri*, probably due to the fact that in Malagasy *indry izy* translates to "there he is."

## Induratize (*v.*) *To harden the heart.*

Among the inevitabilities of old age are that the heart is hardened twice; first figuratively, through experience and loss, and then literally, in the form of atherosclerosis.

*also see:* unlove

## Infelicitate *(v.)* *To cause to be unhappy.*

I have trouble believing I've managed to make it this far in life without a word for describing all the seemingly innumerable ways in which I am made unhappy. *Displease* is close, but doesn't quite work. *Infelicitate* is exactly the word I've been looking for, and with some small dose of irony, it makes me very happy indeed.

## Inquilinate *(v.)* *"To dwell in a strange place."* *(Henry Cockeram,* The English Dictionarie, *1623)*

I once spent a year attempting to live in Southern California. It was there, while reading the dictionary on the beach (a habit for which I was much ridiculed), that I first came across this delightful word. To me, it perfectly describes living in California, and the incomprehensibility of dwelling somewhere where the weather and the general population are matched in vapidity only by each other.

## Insordescent *(adj.)* *Growing in filthiness.*

An obsolete word from the works of the Roman Catholic Church, *insordescent* appears to have been used mostly, if not exclusively, in religious literature. But my life is full of secular instances of things increasing in filthiness, and I intend to keep this word in my pocket and pull it out as needed.

*also see:* nastify

**Inspirado** *(n.) A person who thinks himself inspired.*

A simple rule of thumb: if someone is describing you with a noun that ends in -*o*, chances are, they are not paying you a compliment.

**Interdespise** *(v.) To hate someone as he or she hates you.*

Mutual hatred is not such a bad thing. In fact, many people seem to feel quite comfortable with it. It certainly feels better to hate someone who hates you right back than it is to hate someone who thinks you're a peach.

**Introuvable** *(adj.) Not capable of being found, specifically of books.*

I always have trouble finding my books. I have no system for how my books are arranged; they fit where there is room. Alix has no such trouble, as she color-codes all of her books. On the side of the apartment where her books live are great swaths of reds, yellows, blues, and greens, all blending together neatly. I've tried this system, and it did not work so well, as most of my books are the exact same color—brown and dusty.

*also see:* onomatomania

# J

I'VE ALWAYS BEEN A READER, at least as far back as I can remember. It was most likely my parents' fault, since they employed a form of operant conditioning when my brother and I were young that was designed to make us not want to watch television. It was not expressly forbidden, but the small and crackly thirteen-inch black-and-white TV we owned was kept behind an armchair in the living room, and when we were foolish enough to drag it out the first thing our parents would say was, "Well, if you have enough time to watch TV, then you certainly have enough time to scrub the kitchen floor." After several aborted attempts to watch TV and with a very clean kitchen floor, we more or less gave up on the idea of watching it.

I've always suspected that my parents' reasons for steering us away from TV had mainly to do with the fact that there were four of us living in a small tenement apartment, and if one person was watching TV the rest of the family had no real choice but to be exposed to it as well. Books, on the other hand, could be read without disturbing anyone else. Most evenings from my childhood that I remember consisted of each of the four of us sitting in the living room, either reading our own book, or having a book read out loud.

My parents also had the habit of reading us bedtime stories that were completely incommensurate with our age, and when my brother and I were seven and nine we were being lulled to sleep by Richmond Lattimore's translations of the *Iliad* and the *Odyssey*, Robert Fitzgerald's *Aeneid*, and Malory's *Le Morte d'Arthur*. I don't think they had the intent of educating us young, or believed that we were unduly precocious—they just read what they wanted to read, and we happened to be the ones who were listening.

I bought my first book for myself when I was ten. Stuck at a beach somewhere near the end of Cape Cod one summer, and eventually bored by the normal pursuits of summer, I happened into the clapboard shack by the parking lot that served as a combination of hot dog stand and purveyor of cheap souvenirs. In the back of the store was a shaky wire carousel full of aged paperbacks. They weren't secondhand, just books from twenty years earlier that had never managed to be sold, and the store was letting them go for their original cover prices, twenty-five cents each.

At that age I thought anything that cost a quarter must be a bargain, and I grabbed the first book that caught my eye—*Three Tickets to Adventure* by Gerald Durrell. It was a memoir of sorts, recounting the trials and travails of being an animal collector for zoos in the 1950s.

It was instantly the most transporting experience I could imagine. I had been an avid reader, prone to spending more time while at school in the library than in the classroom, but this was somehow different. Here, fully realized, was the idea that one could just go and find a book that one wanted to read, buy it, and get joyfully and irretrievably lost in its pages.

I suppose it helped that the book I happened upon was humorous and well written (its author to this day remains one of my favorite writers), but more important than that was the idea of escaping into a book. Suddenly it was unclear to me why people bothered to do anything besides read, unless it was of necessity.

I became obsessive about reading, and was not terribly discriminating in my tastes. *Gone With the Wind* interested me every bit as much as *Bullfinch's Mythology*. I would find an author or a genre that seemed acceptable and proceed to shovel everything I could find into my head. I spent three months reading biographies of professional basketball players and then followed that with a spell of reading adventure stories about life in the British navy during the Second World War.

At some point my parents became concerned with the amount of time I spent reading. When I was twelve my father began kicking me out of the house on weekends so that I wouldn't lie on the couch all day with my nose in a book. All this accomplished was to give me the impetus to go out and find new volumes to read. I would walk several miles downtown, to Fifty-fifth Street and Fifth Avenue, where Doubleday had its flagship store. I was more than content to perch on an uncomfortable stool reading all day and then walk home, pretending that I'd been out and about and performing energetic childhood activities for hours.

I've never been prone to buying fancy clothes, or meals in nice restaurants. But I've always allowed myself to buy books, no matter how meager a budget I was living on at the time. Anytime I come across a book that holds the slightest potential that someday I may want to read some part of it I pick it up and bring it home. It isn't a mania for collecting—it's a defense against boredom. The fact that my shelves are filled with things I haven't yet read and want to, and things that I've read before and want to revisit, means I will never be at a loss for entertainment at home.

All of which makes my decision to read dictionaries seem almost logical, as they never fail to interest me, and I can never hope to learn everything that is within even a small one. I often find myself waking in the small hours of the morning, unable to get back to sleep. I suppose if I really worked at it, even for a few minutes, I would be able to return to slumber, but I have no real desire to—there is a room full of books just beyond the door.

The *OED* is the perfect book for these three a.m. moments. It tickles the familiar, telling me once again things about words that I've known for years and forgotten that I forgot. It tells me things that I know I knew about words, but with additional insights that I have blithely ignored over the years. And it tells me things about words that I never could have imagined on my own.

And so three a.m. becomes six, night becomes morning, one cup of coffee becomes four, and the pile of pages shifts from the right to the left as I read my way into the day. In moments like this I am convinced I'll never need another book again.

### Janiform (*adj.*) *Two-faced, resembling Janus.*

Janus, the ancient Roman two-faced god of doorways, appears to have been demoted over the centuries. Although being the god of a doorway may not have had the most social cachet in the pantheon, I imagine it was a step up from being the root of an obscure pejorative term.

### Jehu (*n.*) *A fast or reckless driver.*

Jehu was a king of Israel in the ninth century BCE, renowned for both his furious chariot driving and his extermination of the worshippers of Baal. The use of his name to refer to a reckless driver comes from 2 Kings 9:20: "the driving is like the driving of Jehu the son of Nimshi; for he driveth furiously." Jehu is not the only name from antiquity which has come to be associated with a reckless driver; Phaeton has a similar meaning. In ancient Greek mythology, Phaeton was the son of Helios, and was given the job of driving the sun chariot for a day. From all accounts, he botched the job and Zeus was forced to kill him in order to save the world.

### Jentacular (*adj.*) *Of or pertaining to breakfast.*

Some of you reading this are no doubt thinking, "Why do I need this silly little word that describes 'of or relating to breakfast'?" The answer is you don't need it. But it is also true that you don't need the overwhelming majority of the words you use throughout the day, either, and *jentacular* is far more charming than most of them.

**Jettatore** *(n.) A person who is bad luck.*

Even though he or she is the first person tossed off the life raft when supplies run low, the *jettatore* is not in any way related to *jettison* or *jetsam*.
*also see:* exauspicate

**Jive-ass** *(n.) "A person who loves fun or excitement."* (OED)

Upon first glance I was skeptical of this sense listed for jive-ass, never having known of it being used to refer to a fun person. But then I read on and discovered that the *OED* also states that this is "a word of fluid meaning and application," which sounds to me like a very elegant way of covering one's lexicographic tracks. Perhaps it is a way of saying "Don't come crying to us if this turns out to be wrong—we told you the word had fluid application."

**Jocoserious** *(adj.) Half serious and half in jest.*

*Jocoserious* is in some way an example of itself—it looks like a very serious word, but it's really quite silly.
*also see:* agathokakological

# K

My fascination with words was unintentionally provoked by my eleventh grade English teacher, Mr. Wozniak, a stern man who had a peculiarly large dent in his balding head and a predilection for red plaid shirts. He spoke in a slow monotone and struggled, as I suppose so many English teachers do, with the task of imparting to his students what is and what is not correct English. I cannot say that I remember a great deal of what he taught, or that I had any special opposition to it, except in one area—what counts as a real word.

We were on the subject of homonyms, and Mr. Wozniak dutifully led us through sets of *see/sea*, and *too/two/to*, and then announced that he would give the class a word and ask us to supply its homonym.

"The word is *altar* . . . the word is *altar* . . . can anyone tell me what the homonym for this word is . . . as in: the children worshipped quietly at the *altar* . . . the word is *altar* . . ." Eventually someone raised her hand and supplied the requisite *alter*, and Mr. Wozniak looked mildly pleased. He then proceeded to the next word, which, considering that he was addressing a room of teenagers, was perhaps not the wisest choice of homonym.

"The word is *horde* . . . the word is *horde* . . . as in: the *horde* of Visigoths sacked the city . . . can anyone tell me what the homonym of *horde* is . . . the word is *horde* . . ." Another pause, and then someone mumbled something about a hoard of gold. Another tightly pinched smile from Mr. Wozniak and then he continued. "The word is . . ."

We never got to the next word, as I raised my hand and called out that there was another homonym for *hoard* and *horde*. I wasn't trying to be a smart aleck; I honestly thought that he had forgotten to include the word.

"Another homonym for *hoard*? Hmmm . . . very interesting, Mr. Shea . . . I don't believe I know it—perhaps you could tell us what that word is?"

"The word is *whored*, as in, the squire *whored* his way across all of London," I proudly exclaimed, and then spelled the word, just in case my point hadn't been made. The class tittered predictably, and Mr. Wozniak's face turned an interesting shade of red, except for the dent in his forehead, which stayed white.

"That is *not* a word!" he thundered.

"But—but I just read it last week in—"

"Enough! That is *not* a word!"

# K

Having established that *whored* was not a word, we moved on from homonyms.

This rankled me then, and it rankles me still. How can you say that something people use as a word is not actually a word? It can be a "bad" word, or a slang word, or a substandard or colloquial word; but it is still very much a word. To deny its existence is as wishful and futile as saying that the car that is about to run you over does not exist. And yet this is exactly what many people do when faced with a word they find disagreeable or about which they simply have a vague feeling that it is not "proper English."

One of the ways people frequently claim something is not a word is by asserting that "it is not in the dictionary." The absurdity of this claim is illustrated by the fact that they never actually say what dictionary they are referring to. Hundreds and hundreds of English dictionaries have been published over the past four hundred years, every one of which is somehow different from the others. And none of them can rightfully claim to have absolute authority over what constitutes the language.

Furthermore, dictionaries are not set in stone, nor are they error-free. Even the *OED*, as magnificent a work of scholarship as it is, has plenty of mistakes and inconsistencies. Furthermore, the four-volume supplement to the *OED*, which appeared between 1972 and 1986, includes thousands of words that were not listed in the original version of the *OED*. Does this mean they did not become words until the *OED* supplement printed them? Of course not. When this supplement was being edited, the nonsense words from Lewis Carroll's poem "Jabberwocky" were not included in the first volume, *A–K*. However, after the first volume a decision was made that they should in fact be included, with the result being that any word from "Jabberwocky" that comes after *K* is listed. Thus, *brillig* is not currently in the *OED* but *outgrabe* is. Should this mean that one is a word and the other is not?

I always find it puzzling when I am in conversation with someone who seems to be in many ways intelligent and urbane, yet when faced with a word of dubious provenance, such as *irregardless*, begins sputtering with rage, claiming that the word does not exist.

The *OED* is loaded with words that are not considered "real" (at least by the standards of language purists), and they are great fun to read. While I have no intention of using "words" such as *irregardless*, *happify*, or *fabulosity*, I do enjoy seeing them there on the page, and reading how writers have used and misused them through the ages.


## Kakistocracy *(n.) Government by the worst citizens.*

The *OED* is full of words for different types of governments. I find most of them forgettable. But *kakistocracy*, describing so aptly the fear, which seems common in every generation, that their government is truly the worst possible one, is a word worth remembering.


## Kankedort *(n.) An awkward situation or affair.*

I take comfort in the fact that even when the editors of the

# K

*OED* do not have the answer to something, they manage to impart this lack of knowledge in a particularly graceful fashion, thereby diffusing what would otherwise be a bit of a *kankedort*. The etymology for this word reads "Of unascertained etymology."

*also see:* zugzwang

**Keck** *(v.) To make a sound as though one were about to vomit.*

*Keck* is a good, multipurpose nausea word, for in its various senses it also effortlessly manages to describe "to want to vomit," "to have loathing for," and "to reject food or medicine with loathing."

*also see:* nauseant, vomiturient

**Killcrop** *(n.) A brat who never ceases to be hungry, and was popularly thought to be a fairy that was substituted for the real child.*

This would describe any child other than your own.

*also see:* xenogenesis

# L

I RECENTLY GAVE UP MY APARTMENT and moved in with Alix. She was already in possession of a fine apartment, with a full assembly of furniture, so I decided to get rid of most of my possessions. Except, of course, my dictionaries. Forty-one of the forty-five boxes I moved in with held nothing but dictionaries, and I cannot quite remember what was in the rest.

I spent a week putting up shelves wherever I could find room: an alcove, part of a hallway, the entirety of a closet. As always seems to be the case, there was just enough room to fit the books. But dictionaries are restless creatures, and are never content to just sit there where I've put them.

As a result, the apartment is strewn with dictionaries and their spoor. Piles of books, both small and large, are everywhere. Index cards, stray bits of typing paper, and scraps of whatever substrate was handy at the moment are floating about, dotted with cryptic handwriting and small lists of words.

Alix has borne this proliferation of moldering bindings and paper with remarkable good grace, even though her own small collection of dictionaries is always neatly arranged by her desk. Occasionally she will note that the dictionaries seem to be winning their war with the inhabitants of the apartment, but does not seem to be overly bothered by this.

I've tried to keep my dictionaries ordered and put away, but they never stay put, especially the *OED*. Certain books I can resist browsing, such as the single-volume copy of the *Century Dictionary* (which is over eight thousand pages long and weighs more than my kitchen scale will tolerate), or any of the four volumes of *Cyclopaedia*, Ephraim Chambers's dictionary (which are about a foot wide and a foot and a half tall), but somehow I find myself constantly pulling the *OED* off its shelf. Each of its twenty volumes is of a size that is just asking to be picked up, cradled, and read.

Any of these books can be grabbed and picked up with one hand. When I flop it open my eyes meet with a happy profusion of text, two pages dense with words, no matter what portion of the book I've opened to. The smell of the pages is brimming with learning, evoking both the promise of what has been found already and that which remains to be sought.

The font the *OED* uses has become as recognizable as an old friend. As have the myriad punctuations, symbols, and abbreviations that cover its pages, and which are varied enough to be known in full only to typesetters and longtime readers of this book.

My mornings and evenings are riddled with these sightings of my dictionaries: passing from room to room, I catch a glimpse of some stray volume and remember a word in it that I wanted to revisit. I grab the book and sit down on the floor, the table, or whatever surface is nearby. Instantly I am lost, and happily wending my way through the ages and the alphabet, word after word. I sit there, losing minutes and hours and gaining the world.

## Lant (*v.*) *To add urine to ale, in order to make it stronger.*

The speakers of English have, over the past several hundred years, displayed what seems to be an unreasoning fondness for using urine, both human and otherwise, for a dizzying array of purposes. In addition to *lant*, the *OED* lists such delightful words and terms as *all-flower-water* (cow urine, used as an unspecified remedy), *puppy-water* (the urine of a young dog, used as a cosmetic), and the ever popular *lotium* (stale urine used by barbers). Perhaps their urine was somehow cleaner than the urine of today, just like the music was better, and children were more polite to their elders. It's possible, but my guess is simply that hygienic standards were significantly lower.

*also see:* unbepissed

## Latibulate (*v.*) *To hide oneself in a corner.*

This word may not have much resonance with many people, but given that I spend all day hiding myself in a corner there was no way that I could pass it by.

## Lectory (*n.*) *A place for reading.*

Although I am firmly of the opinion that a book can, and should, be brought along and read anywhere, there can be something almost infinitely pleasing about having a specific place that is designed solely for reading. If you agree with this sentiment you very likely have your own *lectory* somewhere. If you disagree with this sentiment, you are probably not reading this book.

## Leep (*v.*) *"To wash with cow-dung and water."* (OED)

When I came across the definition of *leep* I thought that perhaps the *OED*'s editors had a different understanding of what the word *wash* means. I was moderately distressed when I looked ahead to the *W*'s and found that they have the exact same idea of what it means as I do.

## Leese (*v.*) *To be a loser.*

*Leese* means many different things: to lose (in a variety of senses), to destroy or spoil, to fail to accomplish something, to release or unfasten something. All of these are fine words, but all have synonyms, and add little by way of previously unknown meaning. But it was the second sense of the first definition of *leese* that really caught my eye, as I've seen no other word so far that has been defined as "to be a loser."

## Letabund (*adj.*) *Filled with joy.*

It seems incongruous to me that a word ending in *-bund*

should have such a pleasant meaning. When I think of *-bund* words, I think of words such as *moribund* (at the end of life), *cummerbund* (the end of fashion), and *balkansprachbund* (a grouping of linguistic similarities among the Balkan languages). It's nice to see *letabund* escape its unfortunate childhood and grow up to be such a happy and well-adjusted word.

*also see:* conjubilant, felicificability, happify

## Levament (*n.*) *"The comfort which one hath of his wife."* (*Henry Cockeram,* The English Dictionarie, *1623*)

Of all the lexicographers who are quoted repeatedly in the *OED* (and there are many), it is a toss-up as to whether Samuel Johnson or Henry Cockeram is the more entertaining. On the one hand, Johnson is certainly far superior as a lexicographer, but on the other hand, Cockeram seems to either have found or have made up more absurd and entertaining words.

*also see:* conjugalism

## Lipoxeny (*n.*) *The deserting of a host by the parasites that have been living on it.*

*Lipoxeny* is a very serious and very technical botanical word. Under no circumstances should you ever use it in a manner that is not respectful of the English language and the biologists who worked tirelessly to fill it with words such as this.

## Longueur (*n.*) *A long or boring passage of writing.*

A *longueur* is generally not what one wishes to find in a book, but that is not to say it cannot have its uses. I used to keep by my bed an exceptionally large and ferociously boring book about the history of canned foods, which had been paid for and authored by some council that promoted canned foods in the 1940s. The entire thing was one giant *longueur*, and with its assistance it never took me more than five minutes to fall asleep.

# M

As I read my way through the *OED*, I try to not allow myself to become distracted. This is a difficult task, for a number of reasons. The essential nature of consulting a dictionary is that it is distracting—it is inevitable that one word will remind me of another word I've been wondering about, or will awaken my curiosity as to whether this word and another share an etymological root. And whenever I come across a particularly well-turned phrase in a citation I have to stifle the urge to put the dictionary down and go off to look up whatever book or newspaper it came from so that I might read it in full.

There are other moments in reading the *OED* that cause distraction; and it is not a distraction that comes from a particularly lovely bit of a sonnet by Shakespeare, or from having my interest piqued by an etymology that seems at once wondrous and improbable. It is when I am distracted simply because the definition provided is so absurd that I have to wonder "What on earth were they thinking?" and I feel compelled to stop reading and investigate.

The first such absurdity I noticed was the entry for *cannily*. It is defined, in a single entry, as follows:

*1. Sagaciously*
*2. Skilfully*
*3. Prudently*
*4. Cautiously*
*5. Slily*
*6. Gently*
*7. Softly*
*8. Comfortably*

For good measure, an *etc.* is tacked on at the end of the definition. When reading such a well-respected dictionary my first impulse is to assume I must have missed something. But then I think on it for a while and realize that I simply have no idea what they mean. How can *cannily* mean prudently and comfortably at the same time? If *softly* and *slily* are both listed in the same definition of a word, should I then think of them as synonyms? And what purpose does *etc.* serve in a dictionary—is this James Murray's way of saying "I've supplied you with the first eight meanings of this word; you can make up the rest on your own"?

Later in *C* I discover that *Colubriad* is defined simply as "the epic of a snake." I had no idea that snakes were so advanced that they had gotten around to composing epics, and wonder if they will soon move on to doggerel poetry. Looking further in the entry I can see that this is the title of a work by Cowper in 1782, but no further information is available. I want to put the book down and go look at Cowper, but I feel I don't have the time.

Several letters pass and I discover what is perhaps my favorite definition of all in the *OED*: *disghibelline* ("To distinguish, as a Guelph from a Ghibelline"). When I first read this I was convinced one of the editors had brought his children to work one day, and they amused themselves by creating nonsense definitions for the dictionary, and this one somehow slipped in. This time I could not resist, and went off in search of what Guelphs and Ghibellines are. It turns out they were competing political parties in Italy, a very long time ago, and *disghibelline* is in fact a real definition. When I read it and say it out loud a few times I have the same feeling I get when I discover that the library book I've just taken home has not been checked out in eighty years.

In the *OED* editors' defense, they have set out to accomplish something that is inherently impossible—to record the entirety of a language. It is only natural they should occasionally come across words that are virtually indefinable, or that have meanings that have been lost to the ages. Whatever failings or inconsistencies the editors may exhibit are certainly not for lack of effort. James Murray in particular was renowned for attempting to ferret out knowledge, writing letters to every authority he could think of and posting queries in newspapers begging for information on a word. When I read the definition of *lege de moy* ("App. the name of some dance") I cannot help but imagine that they must have spent a tremendous amount of time looking for the meaning and roots of this word before one of the editors finally threw his hands up in disgust and exclaimed, "What the hell—just say it's some kind of dance or something, and let's get to the pub."

As a reader I never begrudge the *OED* its moments of error or inexplicable oddness. The only thing shocking to me is how infrequently they occur. Quite honestly, I'm relieved when I see the *OED* do silly things on occasion. It humanizes the dictionary, and makes more apparent that this creation is the work of people, not machines. It is fallible, and all the more impressive for it.

## Mafflard *(n.) A stuttering or blundering fool.*

Stutterers have been getting the short end of the stick for thousands of years now, the unfortunate recipients of more misguided attempts at "curing" them than almost any other group, with the possible exception of the left-handed. In the Middle Ages, one theory was that the tongue itself was the problem, and so the logical course of action was, of course, to torture the offending organ with pins and hot irons. So the next time you are faced with a tedious and irritating mafflard, give a thought to the injustice suffered over the ages by stutterers.

## Malesuete *(adj.) Accustomed to poor habits or customs.*

A nice, middle-of-the-road word for describing the common flaws that afflict us all. *Malesuete* does not refer to the catastrophic, hair-pulling, Greek tragedy kinds of flaws, such as being the kind of person who sacrifices his own children. It is more apt for describing things like clipping your toenails in public: the minor flaws that annoy everyone around you.

*also see:* foiblesse, hamartia

## Mammothrept *(adj.) A spoiled child or infant.*

Equipped with a delightful etymology (from the Greek *mammothreptos*, a child brought up by his grandmother), *mammothrept* is a word with a touch of mystery. Its first recorded use is by Saint Augustine, which the *OED* finds puzzling, as Augustine did not know Greek, and in fact had written about his difficulty with the language. It is possible that he took the word from its use in postclassical Latin, a language he was comfortable with.

## Maritality *(n.) Excessive or undue affection on the part of a wife for her husband.*

*Maritality* is used much less than its cognate *uxoriousness* (undue affection for one's wife), although neither one is heard much these days. The adjectival form of the word is the almost familiar *maritorious*.

*also see:* levament

## Mataeotechny *(n.) An unprofitable or useless science or skill.*

That I am able to read dictionaries cover to cover and remember words such as *mataeotechny* is something that everyone I know would agree is unprofitable, most would say is useless, but none would refer to as a skill.

*also see:* chrestomathic

## Materteral *(adj.) Having the characteristics or qualities of an aunt.*

I do not know why *avuncular* (of or pertaining to an uncle) has had such success as a word, and *materteral* has had such a lack of it. In any event, it's probably too late for *materteral* to get into the game now, it's stuck with *consobrinal* (having the relationship of a cousin) on the slag heap of unlucky familial words that no one knows or cares about anymore.

## Matrisate *(v.) To imitate a mother.*

Unlike most of the other words in the *OED* having to do with resembling or imitating a mother, *matrisate* is entirely judgment-free, allowing you to utilize it as you see fit, and without fear of reprisal.

*also see:* novercal, patrizate

## Matutinal *(adj.) Active or wide awake in the morning hours.*

Perhaps the only thing more annoying than someone who

does well with mornings is the person who wants to tell you what the word for this is.

## Mawworm (*n.*) *A hypocrite with pretensions of sanctity.*

*Mawworm* was the name of a character in a 1768 play by Isaac Bickerstaffe.

## Mediocrist (*n.*) *A person of mediocre talents.*

Nobody wants to be mediocre, but someone has to be. In fact, by definition, most people are.

## Microphily (*n.*) *The friendship between people who are not equals in intelligence or status.*

Even though this looks like it should be a happy word I can't help but think of it otherwise. The example that always comes to my mind is in John Steinbeck's *Of Mice and Men*, and we all know how that turned out.

## Micturient (*adj.*) *Having a strong desire to urinate.*

I rarely think this, but I am firmly of the opinion that the *OED* dropped the ball—not with this word, which is admirably defined, but with its cousin: *cacaturient*. In the quote provided for *micturient* both words are used, yet *cacaturient* is not defined in the dictionary. Although it is easy enough to deduce its meaning in this context, I still think it was robbed.

*also see:* pissupprest

## Midlenting (*n.*) *The custom of visiting parents on the fourth Sunday of Lent and giving them presents.*

An old custom that died long ago, *midlenting* has not been in common use as a word for quite some time. I have included it simply as a means of scolding people to visit their parents more often, and to bring presents when they do.

*also see:* storge

## Minimifidian (*n.*) *A person who has the bare minimum of faith (in something).*

To the minimifidian the secret to happiness lies in the doctrine of lowered expectations. Which is not the worst way to go through life; it's hard to be disappointed when you never expect anything.

## Minionette (*adj.*) *Small and attractive.*

It is a good thing I don't much believe our vocabulary is a representation of who we are, else I might have become alarmed at the fact that we have a much greater number of words for large and ugly things, and so few for small and pretty ones.

## Misandry (*n.*) *Hatred of men.*

Although it is not a terribly uncommon word, *misandry* certainly enjoys far less currency today than its partner, *misogyny*. As part of my contribution to rectifying this inequality I propose that we all start using *misandry* whenever the occasion arises.

## Misclad *(adj.) Inappropriately dressed.*

After the definition, the *OED* adds that this word is "also in extended use," a designation I've never been entirely sure about. In this case I choose to interpret it as meaning that *misclad* refers not only to people who dress poorly, but also to those people who dress in a way that is somehow so wrong that one automatically avoids them, such as children who insist on wearing rain gear on sunny days or men under the age of fifty who insist on wearing fedoras.

*also see:* sansculottic

## Misdelight *(n.) Pleasure in something wrong.*

Like many people, I am occasionally struck by the fact that there is a lack of common words in our language for some terribly common thing, such as the habit of taking delight in something that one shouldn't. We all do this; even the saints among us will feel a quiver of excitement and satisfaction when a hated neighbor's house burns down. The *OED* does include *schadenfreude*, a word borrowed from German, which means "to take pleasure in the misfortune of another." But it left out one of my personal favorites, *epicharicacy*, which means the same thing as *schadenfreude*, and was in English dictionaries until the early nineteenth century.

## Misdevout *(adj.) Devout in an inappropriate way.*

A word that is easy to describe loosely, but difficult to define with any great degree of specificity. After all, what is wrongly devout to one man may be perfectly appropriate to another.

*also see:* antinomian

## Miskissing *(n.) Kissing that is wrong.*

There are so many things to kiss improperly and so many ways to do so that I find it impractical that we should have to make do with but a single word to convey all of them.

## Mislove *(v.) To hate; to love in a sinful manner.*

*Mislove* manages the neat trick of having two meanings that are almost opposite each other. While this is not an uncommon phenomenon (for example, *left* can refer to both having departed and remaining), words in this category are usually significantly more boring than *mislove*.

## Monodynamic *(adj.) Having only a single talent.*

The technical word to describe a one-trick pony.

## Moreish *(adj.) Encouraging continued indulgence (said of food or drink).*

Judging by the way it was used in the citations, *moreish* means both wanting to have more because there was not enough in the first place, and wanting more because the first serving was so tasty.

*also see:* bouffage, gramaungere

## Mothersome (*adj.*) *Anxious or nervous in the way a mother is.*

A cynic might notice that there is only one letter difference between *mothersome* and *bothersome*. I, of course, would never draw any parallel between the two.

*also see:* novercal

## Mumpish (*adj.*) *"Sullenly angry."* (OED)

The *OED* notes in its citation for this word that Nathan Bailey defined it slightly differently in his dictionary of 1721—"angry, and silent withal." I am one of those people who sinks into a snittish and quiet funk when I am angry. And as always, I find it distressing when I find an unlovely word that describes me so well.

*also see:* obmutescence

## Mumpsimus (*n.*) *A stubborn refusal to give up an archaism, especially in speech or language.*

I'm not averse to stubbornly clinging to an outdated notion or custom on occasion, and I do not think I would make the argument that our language is improving. But neither would I make the case that things used to be much better back in the time of Shakespeare and Dryden, and I find it puzzling when people insist that our language is under attack by the ravening hordes of ignorance, and will succumb any day now. Why do these people always point to the eras when the majority of the population was illiterate as illustrations of our lost eloquence?

It is as if they are saying, "Ah, we were so much more eloquent before universal education."
*also see:* palaeolatry

## Mysophobia *(n.) An irrational fear of dirt, or being dirty.*

Cleanliness may very well be next to godliness and all that, but when it is taken to extremes it becomes just another terribly annoying trait. Sometimes there's nothing wrong with a little old-fashioned filth.
*also see:* fomes

## Mythistory *(n.) A mythologized account of history.*

In other words: history.

ONE OF THE THINGS that has been painfully apparent as I read through the enormity of the English language is just how very little of it I know. I'll often go through pages and pages without recognizing a single word. Other times I am repeatedly confronted with words I've always felt confident in my knowledge of, only to find that I've been misusing them for years, or that they have other meanings far more interesting than the ones I've been using.

Some days I feel as if I do not actually speak the English language, or understand it with any degree of real comprehension. It is as if I am visiting a foreign country, armed with some silly little tourist phrase book that I've perused for the few weeks before arrival. I may know enough to order a cup of coffee or inquire where the bathroom is, but not much more than that.

These feelings of incomprehension can be traced to several causes. The first is that when you read through a dictionary, and find that you have no idea what a great number of the words mean, it skews your perspective on your own grip on the language. How in the world can I claim to speak English when I'm ignorant of such an enormous amount of its vocabulary? Granted, English is significantly larger than any other language in the world, but still, it would be nice to at least know half of the words in it, and there is no possible way for that to happen.

Also, when I read the dictionary there is no way to keep in order all the words coming through my head. It is like trying to remember all the trees one sees through the window of a train. I lose all sense of what is and what is not a normal word. I'm surprised the *OED* does not list *adoxography* (good writing on a trivial subject), as I remember reading it elsewhere and was looking forward to seeing it here. Then I remember this is not a word that was ever really used by anyone outside of a small handful of lexicographers, and that must be the reason the editors chose to not include it. Although they did decide to include a number of other words that they specify were never in general use, and I regret the absence of *adoxography*.

In a similar fashion I'm both alarmed and amused when I get to *glove*—it seems a strange-looking word, and I find myself wondering why I've never seen this odd term that describes such a common article of clothing, and why the dictionary has devoted such a great amount of space to it. Then I remember what a glove is.

Sometimes I'll go for pages and pages without reading the headwords, only the definitions. Time and again I will read fascinating definitions that turn out to belong to words I had always thought to be pedestrian and boring. The phrase "loyalty to, or partiality for, one's comrades" made me think that the word it defined would be something fairly odd and special, and it of course turned out to be simply *camaraderie*, a word I would never have looked at twice if I happened by it in the street. To be so often intrigued and amazed by the meanings of words that are quite common is something I find both delightful and unsettling. How often in the rest of my life do I fail to pay attention to what words mean?

I'm constantly finding that the former meaning of a word differs significantly from how I know it today. When I learned that *secretary* meant "one privy to a secret" during the fourteenth century I was utterly delighted. And then almost immediately I began scolding myself for not having already realized such an obvious precedent, and thought that I should feel no excitement at discovering something that in hindsight seems so obvious. But it *is* exciting to make these little discoveries about the language, and it shouldn't matter at all if they are obvious to someone else.

For a work that was born out of an era of, and a desire for, scientific exactness, the *OED* has a surprising number of definitions that are poetic in their eloquence. It defines *shut-purse* as "the demon of miserliness," which to my mind reads more like an indication of an editor's grim distaste for misers than it does a strictly accurate definition. This bothers me not at all; I'm happy to see an occasional prejudice injected into the *OED*.

## Nastify (*v.*) *To render nasty; to spoil.*

There is nothing terribly unusual about the meaning of *nastify*; I have included it in this list simply because it looks like a word that would be fun to have rolling off your tongue.

*also see:* insordescent

## Natiform (*adj.*) *Buttock-shaped.*

An obsolete medical term, and one I was surprised to find had never (at least in the citations) been recorded as having been used as an insult.

## Naturesse (*n.*) *A generous act.*

The thing you do for someone when you really, really want something from them in return.

*also see:* storge

## Nauseant (*n.*) *That which nauseates you.*

Some people consider certain foods to be *nauseants*. For others it is things such as travel on a boat or in a bumpy car. For me it is people.

*also see:* vomiturient

## Need-sweat (*n.*) *Sweat from nervousness or anxiety.*

At exactly the moment when you neither need nor want to have sweat dripping and revealing your anxiety (such as when you find your boss standing in your doorway with arms crossed and brow furrowed), *need-sweat* is there for you.

## Nefandous (*adj.*) *Too odious to be spoken of.*

From the classical Latin word *nefandus* (wicked or impious). Some things really are too odious to be spoken of, and so I will not mention them.

*also see:* tacenda

## Neighbourize (*v.*) *To be or act neighborly.*

To some folk, this word may mean stopping by in the evening to share a cup of tea or dropping off a freshly baked apple pie for a new neighbor. To others, it will perhaps mean joining the local school board or the Rotary Club. To me, it reminds me of when my brother and I were young, and "Bananas" Brannick, who lived down the street, overheard my brother speak rudely to our mother. Bananas hoisted him over his shoulder, carried him up to his apartment on the fourth floor, and held him upside down out the window by his ankles, while spanking him and lecturing him on the importance of respect for one's parents. Some people might consider this felonious assault on a minor; I think that in his own way Bananas was just *neighbourizing*.

## Nemesism (*n.*) *Frustration directed inward.*

One of the few words I picked out of the *OED* that is of recent coinage, *nemesism* is the creation of the psychoanalyst Saul Rosenzweig, who proposed in 1938 that the word be used as a counterpart to *narcissism*. He based it on the name of the Greek god of vengeance, Nemesis.

*also see:* idiorepulsive

**Noceur** *(n.) A dissolute and licentious person; a person who stays up late at night.*

We have a needless superfluity of words that mean bounder, cad, libertine, wastrel, whoremongerer, and so on. *Noceur* is differentiated from the rest of the lot by the fact that it seems to be the only one to specify that the rotter in question stays up late at night.

**Nod-crafty** *(adj.) "Given to nodding the head with an air of great wisdom."* (OED)

Always remember that it is better to appear smart than to be smart.

**Novercal** *(adj.) Like a stepmother; stepmotherly.*

From the Latin *noverca* (stepmother), *novercal* has more of a classical sting to it than does *stepmotherly*, and predates that word by several hundred years. In its definition the *OED* notes that this word in extended use also means "cruel, malicious, hostile" and then very helpfully reminds us that such use is frequently derogatory.

*also see:* mothersome

I have recently developed a morbid fear that I am turning into one of "the Library People." If you spend any time at all in public libraries you know what I am referring to. The Library People are not an official or organized group, but you can easily spot them by their noticeable lack of social skills, and they will be found in any major library.

I once spent three weeks in the microfilm room of the Forty-second Street branch of the New York Public Library, reading through every newspaper article published in the *Times* of London over the past two hundred years or so related to fatal accidents. I don't recall exactly why I was doing this; it had something to do with an idea for a book that was mercifully never published. The Forty-second Street branch is the mecca of the Library People, and so I was able to observe them in their natural habitat.

The Library People are typically not homeless, although, like many homeless, they too are often equipped with a large number of plastic bags. These plastic bags usually seem to hold old copies of newspapers, scraps of random paper, and other various and sundry tools of the marginally odd.

As a whole, the Library People are quiet, even reserved, although an outburst of incoherent rage is not uncommon when one discovers that someone else has taken their favorite seat, or a desired book or periodical has gone missing. Aside from these occasional outbursts, which are almost never accompanied by any physical violence, the normal level of social interaction is based largely on mutters and dirty glances.

Although I frequently find myself wondering what they are doing there, I never muster up enough of either the courage or the inclination to approach any of them. In part this is because one of the salient characteristics of the Library People is that they seem to have no more than a nodding acquaintance with the concept of bathing. But I am certainly curious about them, and why they do many of the things they do. Does it help the microfilm machine to work if you curse at it, smack it, or, in moments of great duress, spit on it? Given that you have just come to one of the largest collections of newspaper holdings in the world, is it really necessary to bring an additional eight shopping bags filled with yet more newspapers? Are they really all conspiracy theorists, or do they just imitate them uncannily well?

I wonder what they do at night when the library closes. Do they go home and tend to their own newspaper collections? Several months after I'd spent that time in the microfilm room I happened back one day, and most of the same people who had been there every day previously were still there. Had they ever left? Or was it just coincidence that they happened to be there that particular day, and were they staring at me and wondering the same thing?

So now as I continue wending my way through the *OED* at the Hunter College library I find myself questioning whether I have in fact joined this elusive tribe. I hide in a corner of the basement, reading for eight or ten hours at a stretch. This is nothing unusual in a library, but I seem to have picked up other traits that would place me unwelcomely in the Library People camp. Sometimes I get angry at the dictionary and let loose with a muffled yell, such as when I turn a page and see endless columns of definitions of chemical compounds stretching ahead of me.

I will occasionally talk to the mice that peer out from under the door to a nearby equipment room, looking at me quiveringly and with the anticipation that I am perhaps a source of food, and not merely of curiosity. I tell them to avoid the glue traps, and that Bradley was unfairly thought of as an editor, in my opinion. And after I've sat and read for a few hours I'll have to get up and take a brisk walk through the aisles, swinging my arms, or occasionally take a quick jog up and down the stairs.

When the library opens in the morning I am already there waiting. The clerks and librarians are also already there, and what do they think every morning when they see me go straightaway to the reference desk, add a volume of the *OED* to all the other books and papers that I'm carrying, and scurry furtively down to the basement, leaking bits of scribbled paper?

I may be nominally cleaner than the average Library Person, but I have other accoutrements, such as the twitch in my left eye that has recently developed and the inarticulateness that seems to come with having too many words in my head. I'm not quite dressed for success, since my job is to sit and read a book, and I'm usually attired in wrinkled linen pants and a torn but comfortable shirt, and lacking socks.

One day not long ago I caught a glimpse of myself in a glass door as I shuffled out of the library in search of more coffee. I saw a man with hair askew in all directions, an ink-stained shirt partially untucked, and unlaced shoes, who was talking to himself.

Last night I mentioned to Alix that I was afraid the staff at the library might begin to think I was one of the Library People. She laughed and said that they no doubt already did, and probably had a nickname for me.

## Obdormition (*n.*) *The falling asleep of a limb.*

*Obdormition* is the feeling you get just before *prinkling* (pins and needles).

## Obganiate (*v.*) *To annoy by repeating over and over and over and over.*

This word underwent a curious shift in meaning as it changed languages, as it comes from the Latin *obgannire* (to growl or yelp at). And although I cannot immediately think of anything beyond children in the backseat of a car tirelessly asking "Are we there yet?" I'm sure this word will prove apt in many other areas of life.

## Obligurate (*v.*) *"Prob.: to spend (time) feasting."* (OED)

A word that sounds suspiciously close to *obliterate*, considering that it is referring to such a jovial activity. The *OED* hedges its bets in the definition, prefacing it with the proviso "probably." Personally, I prefer the wording the *OED* cites from an earlier work: "to spend in belly-cheere."
*also see:* residentarian, surfeited

## Obmutescence (*n.*) *The state or condition of obstinately or willfully refusing to speak.*

Anyone who has ever been the parent of, or been related to, or been in the same room with an obstinate child will immediately recognize the behavior defined by this word. On the one hand *obmutescence* can hardly be characterized as a sterling trait, but on the other hand, it is far preferable to a tantrum.
*also see:* mumpish

## Occasionet (*n.*) *A minor occasion.*

If I manage to make it through an entire day without spilling coffee on myself it is an *occasionet*. If I walk into a bookstore after not having visited it for several years and find that the same book I was thinking about buying the last time I visited is still there, it is an *occasionet*. Life is full of small occasions, and with their variety and small joys they somehow seem to be more worthy of celebration than large ones.

## Omnisciturient *(adj.) Desiring omniscience.*

Wanting to know everything might generously be called a very bad idea. You may think you want to know everything, but as you learn more and more you will inevitably discover that there are many things out there you will wish you did not know. If you do not believe me, go find a good-sized dictionary, look up the word *copremesis*, and then ask yourself if you are truly glad that you know more now than you did before.

## Onomatomania *(n.) Vexation at having difficulty in finding the right word.*

Finding a word that so perfectly describes a rather large portion of my everyday existence is one of the things that makes reading the dictionary feel like an intensely personal endeavor. The book is no longer merely a list of words; suddenly it is a catalog of the foibles of the human condition, and it is speaking directly to me. Of course, as soon as I learned this word I promptly forgot what it was, but this just provided me with the frustration of not being able to think of it, and then the satisfaction of once again finding it.

*also see:* acnestis

# O

## Opsigamy *(n.) Marrying late in life.*

Do not confuse the *opsigamist* with the opsimath (a person who begins to learn late in life), as they are of different ilk— the *opsigamist* has obviously not learned anything at all.

## Osculable *(adj.) Able to be kissed.*

Remember, just because someone or something *can* be kissed does not necessarily mean that it should be. Something or someone that can be hugged is referred to as *hugsome*.

## Oxyphonia *(n.) Excessive shrillness of voice.*

People with *oxyphonia* need love, just like everyone else. And I am sure they will get it; they just will not get it from me, as I avoid them like the plague.

# P

WHEN YOU'RE READING THE DICTIONARY, it can be very exciting to find mistakes. Unless you find too many of them, in which case it just means the dictionary you're reading is not a very good one. But should you find an error just once in a great while, it tells you the dictionary you are reading is a very good one indeed, while at the same time you may congratulate yourself for having found an error in such a very good dictionary.

Finding errors in the *OED* (and calling attention to the fact that one has found them) is almost an entire subgenre in the field of lexicography. The first fascicle (*A–Ant*) was published on February 1, 1884. Almost immediately people began writing in with corrections. Less than two months later, the March 22 issue of *Notes and Queries* contained a handful of letters regarding errors both real and imagined. A. Smythe Palmer claimed to have found both a misprint and an etymological error. A reader with the initials W. C. B.

wrote in with a handful of antedatings of words, and W. E. Buckley wrote to complain that neither *aenographies* nor *anarogonick* were included at all. Shortly thereafter, one F. A. Marshall, in a letter published on April 5, made the mistake of merely mentioning, in a parenthetical statement at the end of his letter, that the word *ally-cholly* "appeared to be one of the omissions" from the dictionary.

James Murray was a prodigious letter writer, and an even more prodigious defender of the dictionary (and his work on it). The April 19 issue of *Notes and Queries* printed letters from him addressing the "errors" that were pointed out. To W. C. B. he writes, "I hope that it will be generally remembered that omissions in the *Dictionary* are due not to me and those who *have* worked, but to those who *have not*" and suggests that in future, W. C. B. should mail his antedatings to the dictionary before, and not after, the work is published. Murray took the time to similarly castigate the other letter writers, either for not writing before the dictionary was compiled or for just being wrong.

The letters continued apace, and books on the *OED* began to come out before the dictionary was even finished. In 1920, George G. Loane published a small work titled *A Thousand and One Notes on "A New English Dictionary,"* covering the dictionary as far as it had been completed by that point. Loane's "notes" dealt mainly with antedatings, instances in which he found an earlier example of a word's first use than the *OED* had.

In addition to the many scholars and associations who have worked on this daunting task there are also innumerable unaffiliated individuals who feel the need to contribute their two cents to the lexicographic efforts of the Oxford University Press. Their letters, sprinkled over the last century and some, may be found in the *Times* of London, *Notes and Queries*, and various other publications. I am sure the *OED* has an enormous trove of them as well.

Great dictionaries often attract a good deal of unwanted advice. One of the most famous examples of this was the fury incited by *Webster's Third New International Dictionary* in 1961. For various reasons, a large segment of the dictionary-reading public decided this new dictionary was "permissive" and was helping the language go to a linguistic hell in a handbasket. The offices of Merriam-Webster, as well as newspapers throughout the nation, were inundated with suggestions, some intended to be helpful and others not, as to how the dictionary could be improved.

I'd long wondered why it was that people seemingly felt an irresistible urge to write in with corrections for dictionaries—until I began reading the *OED* and realized what a powerful urge I have, when I find a mistake in the dictionary, to share it with someone. The margins of the ledger I've been keeping all my notes in are full of my own system of shorthand, little squiggles that tell me what to look for when I go back and read through my notes. A word I have a question about has, rather obviously, a question mark next to it. Words that are particularly charming have stars, and sometimes exclamation marks. Random thoughts I've written down are distinguished by arrows pointing at them. It is all very orderly and almost antiseptic. Except when I've come across a mistake. The mistakes are distinguished by a "Ha!": the hubris and excitement

I feel at catching the greatest dictionary in the world in an error is unmistakably apparent.

When I find a simple typo, I get a feeling of minor triumph. When I find something more substantial, such as a misspelled word, I begin to think I should set about applying for a professorship somewhere. And when I find something that is just out-and-out wrong, I'm so proud that I instantly confer upon myself guardian-of-the-language status. However, when I once happened to check some of these entries in the online edition, ones I had so proudly marked as errors, I began to notice something awry as soon as I reached *M*. The editors had corrected all of them, every single error that I'd found from *M* to halfway through *P*. It is a terribly deflating feeling to find out that you were right about something, and that nobody will care.

The *OED* is currently, for the first time in its long and storied history, undergoing a complete edit, which is occurring only in the online version. They started editing at *M*, and have made it partway through *P*, although occasionally a word before or after this will have been edited as well. This may come as a surprise to some, who would naturally assume that it's been furiously edited all along. But it is not so easy to edit a book that is tens of thousands of pages long, and filled with the type of information that is constantly shifting.

Any dictionary ever written is, at least to some extent, already partially obsolete by the time it is published. Even if it takes only a few years to write, some of the words will certainly have changed their meaning slightly during that time, and other new words that didn't make it in will have achieved some prominence in the language. This applies to the *OED* more so than to most dictionaries, as the last fascicle was published forty-four years after the first one. Words such as *appendicitis* and *aeroplane* either did not exist or were thought too scientific to merit inclusion when *A–Ant* was released.

Many of the definitions and other passages in the *OED* are now well over one hundred years old and clearly in need of updating. Thousands of new words have come into the language, and possibly tens of thousands of new uses for existing words. This dictionary is intended to be a historical record, not a museum. Even though I recognize the necessity of these changes, I am sometimes chagrined when I find that the editors have removed something I had a particular fondness for.

A case in point: *ploiter* has long been one of my favorite words. Originally defined in the *OED* as "to work in an ineffective way," it has a playful quality and humor to it. So I was a bit discomfited to see that it has gone missing in the new online edition of the *OED*. Well, "missing" is not quite the right word, but it has certainly been demoted. Where *ploiter* once had its own property as a headword, complete with etymology and citations, now it has been relegated to one of several obsolete alternative spellings of a submeaning of *plouter*. It is as though it has gone from being a country squire with a small but well-laid-out estate to renting a room in someone's basement.

I am sure a good deal of time was put into assessing whether *ploiter* deserved its own headword; technical lexicographic information was weighed, and a reasonable and scientific decision was made. I do not think the editors made a mistake, but I also cannot help but think that something has been lost. Along the same lines, I wish that the new and improved *OED* had not taken the word "pains" out of the etymology for *opera* (it has been replaced with "effort"), since I've always found this art form to be particularly grueling to listen to, and rather liked that I could imagine my prejudices reflected in its roots.

On the other hand, the editing has fixed the mistakes, clarified the order of definitions that have shifted over the years, and added thousands of new words and definitions. Words such as *resistentialism* (describing the seemingly aggressive behavior of inanimate objects) have been added, and I cannot complain about things like that. I can't claim that *ploiter* and *opera* were mistreated, but I'm sad to see their old meanings go.

## Painstaker (*n.*) *One who takes pains.*

The kind of person who is greatly advantageous to have along on a camping trip.

## Palaeolatry (*n.*) *Excessive reverence for that which is old.*

A curious form of nostalgia, extending far back to before when the person who feels it was even born. People who suffer from *palaeolatry* always seem to focus exclusively on the glories of the past, and never get around to mentioning the things that came along with them, such as a life expectancy that was half what it is now, wholesale slaughter, and bimonthly bathing. *also see:* mumpsimus

# P

**Pandiculation** *(n.)* *The act of stretching and extending the limbs, in tiredness or waking.*

Everyone does it, and no one knows what to call it.

**Panurgic** *(adj.)* *Ready for anything.*

Panurge was a character Rabelais created, and he certainly lived up to his name. The roots of it are the Greek words *pan* and *ourgos* ("one who does anything").

**Parabore** *(n.)* *A defense against bores.*

It would be a very lovely thing indeed if there existed some magical device that you could carry around with you to ward off bores. The closest thing to this I have seen is a contraption Alix gave me a few years back: a little black box on a key chain that will turn off every nearby TV with the push of a button. I carried it with me everywhere and used it whenever I came across that particular form of boredom.

**Paracme** *(n.)* *The point at which one's prime is past.*

It is potentially one of the most depressing points in a person's life—the instant they first realize they can no longer do some or many of the things that they formerly could. In other words, the it's-all-downhill-from-here point. However, most of us seem to be equipped with abilities of self-delusion potent enough that we are able to convince ourselves that this is not so for years past the point at which it is true.

**Pathopoeia** *(n.) A passage designed to affect or arouse the emotions.*

The single greatest example of this I can think of is the first movement of Igor Stravinsky's *The Rite of Spring*, which provoked a riot at its first performance in Paris in 1913 among the largely upper-crust attendees.

**Patrizate** *(v.) To take after one's father.*

It seems that whether this is viewed as a good or a bad thing varies from generation to generation.
*also see:* father-better, father-waur

**Pavonize** *(v.) To behave as a peacock might.*

Which either means to flaunt one's appearance in a vain fashion, or to peck at the ground in the hopes of finding bits of food and to clean one's hindquarters with one's mouth.

**Peccability** *(n.) Capacity for sinning.*

It feels inappropriate that *impeccable* (not liable to sin), which is far more rare an occurrence, should so exceed in popularity the word that connotes the converse.

**Pejorist** *(n.) One who thinks the world is getting worse.*

I used to fall prey to the strangely comforting lull of being a *pejorist,* but the more I think about it, the more I realize that the world is pretty much the same degree of horrible it has always been.

*also see:* deteriorism

## Penultimatum *(n.) The final demand before an ultimatum.*

A heady mix of *penultimate* and *ultimatum*, the *penultimatum* is the demand that you set forth when you are too scared of what the possible results of an actual ultimatum would be.

## Peristeronic *(adj.) "Suggestive of pigeons."* (OED)

Although I did spend the better part of a year of my life reading this dictionary, and in doing so lost some of my eyesight and much of my mind, it was certainly not in vain. After all, one cannot put a value on such things as knowing a word that is defined as "suggestive of pigeons."

## Perpotation *(n.) An instance of drunkenness.*

This is one of the words the *OED* does not provide its own definition for, relying instead on the writings of previous lexicographers to tell us what the word means. This practice works well for the most part, but occasionally gives rise to possible misunderstanding. For instance, under the entry for *perpotation* we are told not only that Henry Cockeram defined it in 1623 as "ordinarie drunkenesse," but also that Nathan Bailey defined the same word in 1721 as "a thorough drunkenness." What are we to make of this—that Cockeram was a lush? Or perhaps that Bailey couldn't hold his liquor? It is possible that the word simply changed its meaning in the hundred years between the two books.

## Pertolerate (v.) *To endure steadfastly to the end.*

I am of the opinion that the word *tolerate* should be used to describe enduring life's everyday banalities. *Pertolerate*, on the other hand, as it refers to seeing something through to the bitter end, should be reserved for describing enduring something that is particularly grueling and tiresome, such as musical theater, or performances of any sort by children not your own. *also see:* sitzfleisch

## Pessimum (n.) *The worst possible conditions.*

The anti-Candide word.

## Petecure (n.) *Modest cooking; cooking on a small scale.*

Very few people eat in an epicurean fashion, yet many of them know what the word *epicure* means. A great many people eat in a simple fashion, and yet no one knows the word for this.

## Petrichor (n.) *The pleasant loamy smell of rain on the ground, especially after a long dry spell.*

*Petrichor* is a fairly recent word, having been coined by Isabel Joy Bear and R. G. Thomas for an article they wrote in 1964. I first came across this some six or seven years ago, thought to myself, "What a lovely word," and then promptly forgot what it was. I have spent far too much time since then wondering vainly what it was. When I found it there, buried in the midst of *P*, it was as if a kink in my lower back that had been plaguing me for years suddenly went away.

*also see:* impluvious

## Philodox *(n.) A person in love with his own opinion.*

The *OED* tells us this word is found chiefly in the translations of Montaigne, and it seems rather a pity that this should be so, since *philodox* (coming from the Greek words for "to love" and "opinion") is readily applicable to so many people who have never even heard of Montaigne.

## Pissupprest *(n.) The holding in of urine.*

I do not think this word requires any further explanation from me.

*also see:* micturient

## Plinyism *(n.) "A statement or account of dubious correctness or accuracy, such as some found in the* Naturalis Historia *of Pliny the Elder (AD 23–79)."* (OED)

Here is a word that makes me sad. Not because of its definition, but because of the man whose name it was taken from. Pliny the Elder was a distinguished Roman naturalist, the author of the *Naturalis Historia*, and sounds like an all-around interesting fellow. According to his nephew, he died during the eruption of Vesuvius because he wanted to stay to watch the volcano and help those in need. Yet in the *OED* his name is forever linked with error. Why? Because in 1702 a bitter small man by the name of Cotton Mather did not much care for Pliny and coined this word. Mather seems to have been the only person ever to have used the word, yet sometimes that is enough to gain entry into the annals of language, rightly or wrongly. Perhaps there should be a related term, something along the lines of *mather*, say, which would mean "to attack a writer of far greater stature than oneself."

## Postferment (*n.*) *One's removal to an inferior office. As opposed to* preferment.

No, this word does not refer to having your desk moved out of the corner suite with the window and into the janitor's closet. It is close in meaning to *demotion*, but with a somewhat broader connotation.

## Postreme (*n.*) *He who is last.*

Although it also functions an adjective and an adverb, the appeal of *postreme* lies in the fact that you can use it to refer to a person. While it is true that the word is not defined with the notion of insulting someone, that doesn't mean you cannot utilize it in such a fashion. After all, a word like *postreme* can describe the person who comes in last place, or is picked last, or is just generally lagging behind the rest of humanity. In other words, it is the technical term for "loser."

*also see:* leese

**Postvide** (*v.*) *To make plans for an event only after it has occurred.*

As opposed to *provide*, the original meaning of which the *OED* defines as "to make provision for beforehand; to take measures to ensure that something shall not happen." *Postvide* is the much less known and much more common antonym of this word.

**Pot-fury** (*n.*) *Excitement or anger from drunkenness.*

*Pot* has been used to describe the mood-alterer that one drinks far longer than it has been used to refer to the one that is smoked (sixteenth century versus early twentieth century). *Pot-fury* is just one of a host of words in which liquor has had a hand.

Pot-meal—*a drinking bout.*

Potpanion—*a drinking companion.*

Pot-punishment—*the punishment of being forced to drink.*

Pot-sure—*bold or confident from the effects of alcohol.*

Pottical—*full of, or inspired by, alcohol.*

*also see:* well-corned

**Preantepenult** (*adj.*) *Not the last, not the one before the last, and not the one before the one before the last. The next one.*

A sterling example of how it often can be far more confusing to use one word than several. It is far easier to say "the third from the last" than *preantepenult*.

**Prend** (*n.*) *A mended crack.*

A pithy word that gets right to the point, and serves its purpose admirably, describing something for which I know of no other word. Sometimes I find myself wishing that our whole language was made up of these handy and monosyllabic words.

## Propassion (n.) *The initial stirrings of a passion.*

*Propassion* comes from the postclassical Latin *propassio*, which the *OED* defines as a feeling that "precedes or anticipates desire or suffering." Most of the uses of *propassion* are ecclesiastic in nature, and the passion referred to in the definition typically has more to do with "the Passion of the Christ" than it does the passion of the boudoir.

## Psithurism (n.) *The whispering of leaves moved by the wind.*

Perhaps *psithurism* does not sound like a beautiful word to you, or as though it would describe a beautiful thing. But even a crank like me cannot resist the gentle rustling of autumnal leaves in a breeze, and every time I think of this word it brings that pleasing sound into my head.

*also see:* undisonant

## Psittacism (n.) *The meaningless or mechanical repetition of words or phrases.*

Although I had long thought that parrots and college students who have just begun taking classes in literary theory were the main sufferers of this malaise, I have recently come to realize that it afflicts just about everyone.

Shortly after running into a friend of mine who re-marked that I look somewhat more sallow than he remembered, I decide I need to get out of the library basement. It is the middle of summer, and I have spent almost all of it, and the entirety of spring, in the corner of a subterranean and windowless room. I haven't quite felt that I am missing anything; I've always consid-ered summer to be the most overrated of the seasons, a nasty vul-gar affair during which people feel compelled to visit places I don't want to go (like the beach) and do things I don't want to do (like swim and relax). And yet I don't want to become too much of a re-cluse, and perhaps the fresh air will clear my head as I read.

After all, one of the joys of reading is that you can do it almost anywhere. I always have a book with me anyway, for those mo-ments such as when the train arrives late, or is on time, or doesn't show at all. I resolve to begin visiting other places to read, places that share none of the characteristics of where I have been reading—places with no fluorescent lighting, Formica desks, or low ceilings.

My first attempt is a small park at the easternmost end of Fifty-seventh Street. It's a pleasant little patch, large trees overhead and what seems to be a perpetual and gentle breeze blowing through. There is shade, and a number of moderately comfortable benches to sit on. Best of all, it overlooks the wide expanse of the East River, and occasionally an enormous ship floats by.

This seems almost ideal at first. It is outside, but quiet. I can read largely uninterrupted, and whenever the urge strikes me I can take my eyes from the page and look across the river. Sometimes it's nice to look at things that are far away.

I enjoy a full two hours of reading in my bucolic urban oasis before the baby carriages begin arriving.

Perhaps some people can in fact read in a small park full of screaming children—I am not one of them. I guess I shouldn't be surprised—after all, it is a children's park. But it sounds less like a park than a place to which parents bring their children in order to teach them how to scream. I beat a hasty retreat to my library basement and spend the rest of the day sulkily reading.

The next weekend I decide to venture somewhat further afield, and take the train under the river and across to New Jersey. Hoboken has a number of pretty riverfront parks, some of which stretch, pierlike, far out into the river. I arrive there early on a Sunday morning and set myself on a bench near the water. It initially seems like a lovely place to read, just as the park on Fifty-

---

seventh Street did. Boats meander toward the bay, birds lazy to and fro, and of course, the glory of Manhattan stretches down the skyline. And no screaming children are in sight.

As it turns out, the children are not necessary, as the wind does a more than satisfactory job of making reading impossible. The only way I can read without having the pages whipped back and forth by what seems like a petulant gale is if I turn my back to Manhattan and the river, shielding the *OED* while crouched over. Aside from being an uncomfortable position to sit in, this also means that when I look up all I see is a row of nasty little condominium towers, composed of wan brown brick and promising midlevel elegance. I finish the coffee I brought with me and rush back to the island of Manhattan.

Another week of reading in the library, another week of shushing college students, another week of reading to the hum of intermittently working fluorescent lighting, and I am ready to give reading outside another try. This time I go to Central Park, and after bicycling around for some while, I settle on a bench by a small boat pond.

It doesn't work. There is no wind, and no screaming children. The weather is lovely, and at this early hour of the morning there are barely any people around. There is nothing wrong here; I just don't like it as a spot to read. There are too many minor distractions—a dog runs by and pauses to sniff at my feet, a car honks somewhere in the distance, a jogger struggles by with labored breath. The world manages to intrude on my reading in a thousand small and unintentional ways.

---

Suddenly I'm aware that it doesn't have to be so. I do not need to waste any more time in windy, noisy outdoor settings. Another of the joys of reading a great book is that the world at large is rendered superfluous for the time you spend reading. You do not need to bring the book out into the world—the world comes to you, through the book.

Now that this has been settled, I pack the *OED* back into my bag and return to my library basement, happy and content to reach out to the world, at least for now, through the pages of the book in my lap.

Even though I am somewhat buoyed by my newfound comfort in reading in isolation in my library basement, I have to say that *Q* has been a disappointment. I'm not sure why, but I'd been approaching this particular letter with a great deal of anticipation. Even though I've read through *Q* in a number of other dictionaries and don't recall ever being bowled over, I still had this feeling that it would be full of wonderful and interesting words that somehow had previously escaped my notice.

Additionally, the twitch in the small muscles of my left eyelid has been getting steadily worse. And the recently found knowledge that the word *muscle* comes from the Latin word *musculus* (from the word for mouse, supposedly because the movement of a muscle resembles that of a small mouse running underneath the skin) does nothing at all to make the twitch any less annoying.

*Q* is a boring letter, and I cannot in good conscience recommend that anyone buy the entire *OED* just to read it. The best thing to come out of *Q* is that during the reading of this letter I

# Q

realize that most likely I will not lose my mind, perhaps because the section is so short that it gives me hope.

Perhaps twenty or twenty-five words are included that begin with a *q* not immediately followed by a *u*. If you are a Scrabble player and hunting for words such as these to baffle your opponents, do not read *Q* in the *OED*. Most of those non-*qu* words are not recognized by the Scrabble dictionary, and you will just lose your turn if you try to put them on the board.

### Quaesitum *(n.) The answer to a problem; the thing that is looked for.*

It is a proven fact that if you use a big fancy word like *quaesitum* to describe your silly everyday problems it will be much more satisfying to solve them. At least that's what I've heard.

### Quag *(v.) To shake (said of something that is soft or flabby).*

Why is it that the most powerfully evocative words almost always evoke powerfully unpleasant images? The *OED* specifies that *quag* is an onomatopoeic word, which I find terribly disturbing.

### Quaresimal *(adj.) Said of a meal, having the qualities of food served during Lent; austere, skimpy.*

*Quaresimal* is one of more than a hundred words listed in the *OED* for which James Joyce has provided the first citation. Other noteworthy words he coined include *impotentizing*

(describing that which makes one impotent), *pelurious* (hairy), and *smellsip* (to smell and sip at the same time).
*also see:* bouffage

## Queaning *(n.) Associating with women of immodest character.*

At moments like this, when I see the *OED* clucking about associating with immodest women, I remember that a great deal of what I'm reading in it was actually written over a hundred years ago.

## Quisquilious *(adj.) Of the nature of garbage or trash.*

From the Latin *quisquilae* (rubbish, trash), *quisquilious* is quite a fancy word for such a decidedly unfancy concept. I would enjoy it if more of our vocabulary did not match up with its meanings, and things of effervescent beauty were described with words such as *skrug* and more unpleasant things were described by words such as *quisquilious*.

## Quomodocunquize *(v.) To make money in any way possible.*

A number of the odd and fantastic words in the *OED* seem to have been either first used or popularized by Sir Thomas Urquhart. When reading the citation of his that the *OED* uses to illustrate this word, it is hard for me to understand why we do not commonly use more of his favorite words. Even if you have no real idea what his meaning is, the sentiment is unmistakable and beautifully indelible: *"Those quomodocunquizing clusterfists and rapacious varlets."*

# R

ONE EVENING, WHILE I AM ENJOYING the end of *R* and dreading the beginning of *S*—by far the letter with the most *OED* entries—I get a phone call from my friend Madeline, the dictionary collector. She is calling to tell me about the biannual conference of the Dictionary Society of North America, taking place the next week at the University of Chicago, and wants to know if I will be going.

Perhaps few people would receive notice of a dictionary society meeting with considerable excitement; I, clearly, am one of those people. Besides, I desperately want to take a break from reading. But I don't feel I can afford to take the time off from my reading, and I have some momentum going. I fear that if I stop reading, even for only a week, coming back to the sea of *S*'s when I return might prove to be too demoralizing for me to continue.

I have been having dreams about words lately, a sign that would seem to indicate that I need to take some sort of hiatus from the project. The dreams are not fantastic, nor are they nightmares: their entirely pedestrian nature is what makes them so disturbing. I wake in the middle of the night with a start and the terrible feeling that accompanies a dream in which you think you've forgotten something that is very important. And then I hear a deep voice resonating unbidden in my mind, enunciating some word or definition I thought I'd forgotten. I do not view this as a sign of progress.

Then I take at look at the schedule for the conference, and the list of lectures that will be given, and I realize this will be the perfect way to take a vacation without feeling as though I am wasting any time. Not only are there going to be lectures that any bona fide dictionary lover would drool over, such as "Care and Feeding of a Corpus" and "Considered and Regarded: Indicators of Belief and Doubt in Dictionary Definitions," but there will also be a number of lexicographers from the *Oxford English Dictionary* attending.

Aside from feeling the allure of a guilt-free working vacation, I want to go simply because I think it will be pleasant to be around a large crowd of people for whom reading dictionaries is not viewed as a morbid proclivity. I imagine that I will meet any number of elderly men and women at the conference who will nod their heads fondly and say something along the lines of "I remember the first few times I read the *OED* . . ."

So I buy myself a plane ticket to Chicago and a few days later find myself flying into O'Hare Airport at eight in the morning. Things immediately start on the right note when the woman at the check-in counter gives me a canvas tote bag with "The Oxford

English Dictionary" emblazoned on it, and then directs me to the enormous coffeepot in the basement.

The first thing I notice about my fellow attendees is that an alarmingly large number of them wear bow ties. The next thing I notice is that very few of them are not lexicographers or academics. In fact, I only notice three of us who are attending purely as fans: two of whom are Madeline and myself.

The lectures are incredibly entertaining. I've been reading almost naught but dictionaries and books and papers about dictionaries for the past decade, and many of the people whom I've only known as names on a title page are there. I restrain myself from asking for autographs from several lexicographers whose work I much admire.

On the second day of the conference I meet Sidney Landau, who is one of the preeminent writers on lexicography today and has long been one of my favorite writers on the subject. Not only was he formerly the editor in chief for the *Random House Dictionary of the English Language*, he is also the author of *Dictionaries: The Art and Craft of Lexicography*, which is a terribly important book for a guy like me.

Landau is both witty and erudite, and seems only slightly surprised when I tell him I am a big fan of his. Several minutes into our conversation his eyes suddenly narrow and he says in an almost accusatory tone, "I've heard that you are reading the entire *OED*." I respond that this is true, and he says, "But that's mad!"

This is not quite the reaction I'd have expected from a man who has spent the last four decades writing dictionaries, a man who prepared the latest edition of a book he'd written by retyping the entire previous edition by hand, in order to refamiliarize himself with the material. But it turns out to not be an uncommon one. When I meet another member of the Dictionary Society and tell him what I am doing, he chuckles and says, "Ha! That's quite funny . . . you know, for a moment there I thought you said you were going to read the whole—what?—but—but—but it's so long!"

This is admittedly nonplussing. I had been certain I was going to be in the midst of a group of people for whom my only oddity was not that I was reading the *OED* (this would surely be commonplace), but rather that I'd decided to write a book about doing so.

For a brief period of time I find myself wondering if what I am doing is so abstruse that even the lexicographers think I am a nerd.

This concern does not last long; in fact it is later that afternoon as I am listening to a paper presented by one of the lexicographers from Oxford that I have a change of mind. A woman named Sarah Ogilvie is talking about how she has spent a good deal of the last five years trying to unearth the reason that a particular form of punctuation (//), called tramlines, and used to designate a word that has not yet been naturalized, is missing from the supplement to the *OED*. She has not yet gotten to the bottom, but she is close, and expects to know fully what the reason is within another year or two.

Five years looking for a missing punctuation mark: I am filled with admiration and jealousy. The *OED* is full of mysteries, and I don't yet have the time to chase after all the questions I have about it. But sometimes I would love to stop my constant movement forward, to cease feeling as though I have to get to the next letter, to put the book down and look for the answers to some of these other lingering questions.

While the searcher for the missing tramlines may be an extreme example, she is by no means the only person here who has devoted an enormous amount of time to ferreting out an answer to a question that very few people even know exists; in fact, the conference turns out to be full of them.

I understand why none of the people I've met have read the whole *OED*; they are all too busy looking at or compiling other dictionaries. Who has the time to read a twenty-volume dictionary when you have to finish writing your own? Feeling simultaneously abashed and relieved, I realize that I am, in every sense of the word, an amateur.

The conference lasts only three days, and I am tremendously saddened to see it end. It has been a refreshing change to feel as though I am still immersed in a dictionary, but in a somewhat social fashion, and the lexicographers, linguists, and assorted oddball scholars who make up the DSNA are a far more interesting group than I had expected them to be. But as always when I travel, there is a palpable excitement to get home. Just a short plane ride away is my New York, my girlfriend, my dictionary, and all the other things, small and large, that make life so enjoyable. Some of them alphabetized.

**Rapin** (*n.*) *An unruly art student.*

I do not think I know any art students at the moment, and I am certain I do not know any unruly ones. But should I have occasion to meet any in the future I will be armed with the appropriate thing to call them.

### Recray (*v.*) *To yield in a cowardly fashion.*

I do not know why the Old French *recroire* (to yield in trial by combat) has turned into the English *recray*, with its accusations of cowardice, but I'm sure that with just a little effort we can figure out a way to blame it on the French.

### Recrudescence (*n.*) *The reappearance of something, usually regarded as bad.*

*Recrudescence* is a medical term (which I have seen elsewhere defined as "the reappearance of something bad"). The word was rather oddly redefined by the brothers Fowler in 1906 in *The King's English*, and used in the sense of "the reappearance of something good."

### Redamancy (*n.*) *The act of loving in return.*

*Redamancy* is distinguished from most of the other words about love in that it is one of the few that specifies reciprocity. *also see:* unlove

### Redeless (*adj.*) *Not knowing what to do in an emergency.*

*Redeless* has a variety of meanings, but this is the one that speaks to me the most. In yet another case of the rare thing enjoying a common word and vice versa, it is interesting to note that *redeless* has largely (or entirely) fallen by the linguistic wayside, while *savoir faire* (which originally meant "knowing what to do in an emergency") has survived.

## Redonation *(n.) The action of giving something back.*

*Redonation* first appears in the early seventeenth century, which would lead me to believe that people have been giving useless junk as wedding presents for at least four hundred years now.

## Rejoy *(v.) To enjoy something as its possessor.*

*Rejoy* has several meanings, the first two of which are somewhat noble, and more than somewhat boring. The third meaning, however, is probably the most applicable one for most people, as so many of us cannot seem to enjoy things unless we possess them. Which explains the existence of shopping malls.

## Remord *(n.) A touch of remorse; (v.) to remember with regret.*

Like *rejoy*, *remord* enjoys a wide variety of meanings, but the two listed above leaped out at me. The first of these manages to make remorse sound something like a bit of milk being added to your tea. But when utilized as a verb, *remord* seems as though it can instantly render poetic any decision made in the past and subsequently regretted, from the choice you made twenty years ago to not say something to that young woman on the train in Switzerland, to the choice you made last night to finish that third gimlet.

*also see:* desiderium

## Repertitious *(adj.) Found by chance or accident.*

*Repertitious* has not had nearly the success in entering the language that *serendipitous* has had, most likely because its PR team isn't nearly as good. The noun form of the latter, *serendipity*, was made up in the 1750s by the novelist Horace Walpole, based on Serendip (a former name for Sri Lanka). *Repertitious*, on the other hand, has its first mention in Thomas Blount's dictionary of 1656. Writers—1, lexicographers—0.

## Resentient *(n.) A thing that causes a change of feeling.*

It could be the way that he chews or the fact that he always interrupts you. It could be the embarrassing way that she laughs, or the fact that she snores loudly and will not admit it.

*also see:* aeipathy, unlove

## Residentarian *(n.) A person who is given to remaining at table.*

One of the greatest *residentarians* of all time was Diamond Jim Brady, the famed financier and glutton of the Gilded Age. Brady was fond of fine jewelry, fine meals (fourteen courses at a sitting), and Lillian Russell. When asked how he knew when he'd had enough to eat, he is reported to have answered that he would start his meal with three or four inches between his stomach and the table, and when the two began to rub together tightly he'd stop.

*also see:* obligurate, surfeited

## Resipiscence *(n.) A return to a better state of mind or opinion.*

The reason for the birth of the preprandial drink.

## Rhypophagy *(n.) The eating of filth or disgusting matter.*

The citations for this word include the extremely helpful advice from the *Daily News* in 1881, stating that "*Rhypophagy* is not, on the whole, a healthy practice." The inclusion of the phrase "on the whole" would imply that there may be some circumstances in which the eating of filth is in fact a healthy practice. Bear in mind that this was written in nineteenth-century London, where street vendors sold such delicacies as meat pies of indeterminate origin.

## Roorback *(n.) A flash report that is circulated for political purposes.*

The old saw "The more things change, the more they stay the same" applies to most areas of life, and politics is certainly among them. This word became synonymous with foul play in politics during the 1844 presidential campaign, when a letter from a man supposedly named Baron von Roorback was sent to a newspaper in upstate New York, claiming that one of the men running for office, James K. Polk, had been keeping slaves and branding them. The letter was soon proved to be a fake, Polk entered the White House, and *roorback* entered the lexicon.

**Rough music** (*v.*) *To annoy a neighbor by creating a loud noise, such as through knocking pots and pans together.*

Pots and pans were apparently quite popular at one point as noise-making devices. On a related note, the *OED* also lists *ran-tanning*, the practice of publicly shaming a man who has beaten his wife, by standing outside his residence and banging away on pots, pans, and other assorted objects.

**Rubicundity** (*n.*) *"Redness (of face) from good living."* (OED)

A quick translation: what the *OED* refers to as "good living" we typically call "cirrhosis of the liver."

**Rue-bargain** (*n.*) *A bargain that one regrets, or breaks.*

A good honest English dialectical term for a deal with the devil.

**Ruffing** (*n.*) *The stomping of feet as a form of applause.*

Maybe you do not go through life as I do, plagued by things for which I think "There's a word for that and I can't remember what it is" or "There must be a word for that, and I haven't found it yet." This is a constant and slow irritation, an itch somewhere in the back of my brain, and can sometimes be so overwhelming that it disrupts my ability to speak. The only balm for this is to discover brilliant words like *ruffing*.

# S

ONE OF THE REASONS THE *OED* is so wonderfully and excruciatingly long is the thoroughness with which it treats almost every word. Nowhere is this more apparent than in *S*, which stretches across four of the twenty volumes and takes up more than three thousand pages. It is full of common words that are meticulously dissected, where every possible meaning is considered, and which can be quite painful to read. But whatever difficulty I might have in reading a word, I imagine that defining it in the first place was significantly more difficult, and I wouldn't feel right about skipping over something that some long-suffering lexicographer spent so much time and effort on.

Many people believe that the best dictionary is the one with the greatest number of difficult words in it. While the treatment of hard words certainly does matter, I think that a much better indication of what makes a dictionary great is how it treats the most common words of the language.

For example, let's look at what might be referred to as a hard word—*pneumonoultramicroscopicsilicovolcanokoniosis*. Yes, it is big and imposing, with forty-five letters and nineteen syllables, but it only has one meaning (it's a kind of lung disease). Once you discover what that one meaning is . . . well, that's it, the word is defined and dismissed.

This business of writing a dictionary suddenly doesn't seem so difficult—find a word, write down what it means, alphabetize it, and then call it a day and congratulate yourself for having recorded the language so successfully.

By contrast, let us next look at what might be referred to as a common word—*go*. Everyone knows what *go* means, and one might be forgiven for thinking that if a monster like *pneumonoultramicroscopicsilicovolcanokoniosis* was easy to define, then *go* should be much, much easier. But is it? Actually, it is almost impossible.

A word like *go* doesn't have just one meaning—it can have dozens and dozens of them. A child might have to *go* (to the bathroom), or have a *go* (a turn in a game), or play *go* (a Japanese board game), or simply want to *go* (to leave). There are many other meanings of *go*, and that's before you get to its role in combinations and phrases, all of which also need to be defined. You can *go* crazy, *go* short, *go* wide, *go* with, and, my personal favorite, *go* the vole (in cards, to take great risks in the hopes of great gain).

If this still doesn't seem so difficult, feel free to stop reading this book for a spell and have a *go* at defining a common word of your choice—a short, simple one that you use all the time. How about . . .

*Set.*

Go ahead and try to define *set.* Write down everything you can think of about this simple little word. Jot down every meaning you can think of, and then compare your list of meanings and senses of *set* with the one that's in the *OED.*

Exhaustive is not quite the right word to describe the *OED*'s definition of *set,* as it is the length of a novel, taking up more than twenty-five pages in the *OED. Set* is the largest entry in the print version of the *OED* (it has been usurped by *make* in the online *OED,* but only because *M* has already been revised and added to, and *S* has not). It is broken down into hundreds of senses, and most of those senses have various subgroupings that distinguish it even further. This is a word you can spend a week or more wallowing in. You can roll around in there and lose sight of what language actually is as your mind struggles to differentiate among the hundreds of shades of meaning that can be produced by three letters.

You should read it.

I'm serious; you should read it, all sixty-thousand–odd words of it. In fact, if you do not own the *OED* you should go out tomorrow and buy it, just so that you can read this one definition. If you won't buy it you should go to the library, or to the house of a friend who owns the *OED.* Invite yourself in, curl up in your friend's favorite armchair, and proceed to spend the next few days reading.

To give you an idea of how comprehensive the definition of this word is, consider that, as a verb, it has 155 main senses listed, some of which (such as *set up*) have as many as seventy subsenses. *Set* functions not only as a verb, but also as an adjective (nine main senses), a noun (forty-eight main senses), and a conjunction (one sense).

*Set* can have as commonplace a definition as "a grudge," as poetic as "the end of life," and as pedestrian as "a mining lease." Its use stretches from well over a thousand years ago to the present, an astonishing degree of longevity.

More than two dozen of Shakespeare's plays are quoted in illustrating *set*. Other works cited range from the magnificence of Tennyson, Austen, and Chaucer to the slightly more obscure, such as the line from Sir Richard Steele's 1702 work *The Tatler*: "The new Man has broke his Leg, which is so ill set, that he can never dance more."

Before I exhort you any further to go out and read this *OED* entry in its entirety, I should perhaps mention that it took me three attempts before I was able to read it fully. And after the third attempt, when I had finally succeeded, did I feel a surge of triumph or accomplishment? No, I felt like I was going to vomit, and sat in the library with my head poised over the wastebasket for some time before the urge passed. It is admittedly a great deal of information on a single word, and I would not blame anyone for not wanting to read the whole thing.

But one of the things that irks lexicographers the most is that the common words—the ones that require the greatest expenditure of effort to define—are the same words that are looked up the most infrequently. However, anyone can sit down and leaf through *set* without any undue fear of overdosing on the definition. If you are not interested in reading it for your own edification then you should read it as a silent tribute to all the lexicographers who slaved away for untold thousands of hours crafting this very long definition for this very short word.

### Safety-firster (*n.*) *A person who is unwilling to take risks.*

One of the many joys of reading the *OED* lies in tracing the way a word or phrase will change over the course of time. The expression "Safety first" apparently came about in the nineteenth century in the American railroad industry, and was adopted in Britain by a number of campaigns that were seeking to improve safety in various areas. In the early twentieth century there is a quote telling of corporations that have adopted this slogan and admiringly says that they "have done great work in accident prevention." Other quotes from that era are similarly laudatory.

But soon enough it is clear that the meaning of this expression is shifting. Agatha Christie wrote in 1936, "The moment you begin . . . adopting as your motto 'Safety First' you might as well be dead." Other quotes from this era begin to use the term *safety-firster*, and by now it has gone from being a byword for conscientious and watchful to being listed in the *OED* as describing some variety of coward.

### Salvo (*n.*) *An intentionally bad excuse.*

As opposed to the current common meaning of *salvo* (a firing of artillery), this older sense refers to the excuse you give your boss when you are trying to get yourself fired.

## Sansculottic *(adj.) Clothed inadequately, or in some improper fashion.*

All the world knows of the *sansculottes* ("without knee breeches"), the militant participants in the French Revolution. It is oddly sad that their name went from inspiring fear and awe to becoming a way to describe a guy who ought to put his shirt back on.

*also see:* debag, misclad

## Sarcast *(n.) A writer or speaker who is sarcastic.*

Like *sarcasm, sarcast* comes from the Greek *sarkazein* (to tear flesh like dogs).

## Sardonian *(n.) "One who flatters with deadly intent."* (OED)

The *OED* explains that this word comes from the Latin term for the "Sardinian plant" (*herba Sardonia*), which purportedly killed those who ate it, after producing in them convulsions that appeared to mimic laughter.

*also see:* elozable

## Scrouge *(v.) To inconvenience or discomfort a person by pressing against him or her or by standing too close.*

For passengers of modern transportation everywhere, this word has tremendous and unfortunate resonance. It falls firmly within the category of words that one wishes one did not have occasion to use on a daily basis, but are fascinating nonetheless.

## Scrupulant (*n.*) *A person who is overly conscientious about confessing his or her sins.*

Nobody likes people who are too eager to confess each and every one of their sins; it becomes tedious after a while, even to the clergy. This is powerfully emphasized by the citation for this word, taken from the *Journal of Theological Studies* in 1961, which stresses that when dealing with a *scrupulant* one should "persuade him of the pathological element of his personality."

## Selfist (*n.*) *A person who is selfish or self-centered.*

*Selfists* are nasty little people—it is fitting that they should have a nasty little word to describe them.

## Semese (*adj.*) *Half-eaten.*

To say you'll be serving *semese* sounds so much less appetizing than to declare it leftovers night.

## Sequacious (*adj.*) *Prone to following the thoughts and opinions of others in a fashion that is slavish and unreasoning.*

Common in the seventeenth century, and still used in the eighteenth and nineteenth, *sequacious* appears to have been largely absent over the past hundred years or so. The behavior it describes remains unfortunately all too common.
*also see:* psittacism

**Sesquihoral** *(adj.) Lasting an hour and a half.*

Because sometimes you just don't feel like saying "an hour and a half."

**Short-thinker** *(n.) One whose thoughts do not carry him far into a subject.*

*Short-thinkers* really shine at cocktail parties, and not much else.

**Shot-clog** *(n.) "An unwelcome companion tolerated because he pays the shot for the rest."* (OED)

I have seen this word defined elsewhere as being specifically someone who is tolerated because he or she is paying for the drinks. The *OED* seems to define it in a broader sense, but in any event everyone should know at least one or two *shot-clogs*.

**Sialoquent** *(n.) "That spits much in his speech."* (*Thomas Bount*, Glossographia, *1656*)

One wants to feel pity for the sialoquent, for he typically is unaware that his words are borne aloft by chariots of his own sputum, but it is a difficult thing to do, particularly if he happens to be standing within spitting distance.

**Silentiary** *(n.) An official whose job it is to command silence.*

I would like to have my very own *silentiary*, someone I can bring to the library and to the apartment next door.

## Sitzfleisch (*n.*) *The ability to endure in some activity.*

I am always careful to pack a can of *sitzfleisch* whenever I have to go to the post office or visit a friend who wants to show me his entire collection of baby pictures.

*also see:* pertolerate

## Solivagant (*n.*) *A person who wanders about alone.*

The citations for *solivagant* create a portrait of a lone walker who is a tramp or vagrant. Which reminds me of when I lived in Southern California, a car culture capital, and didn't know how to drive. At first I was offended that drivers looked askance at me as I made my way around town on foot, until I realized that the only other walkers in Southern California seem to be either indigent or insane.

*also see:* vicambulist

## Somnificator (*n.*) *One who induces sleep in others.*

Just what everyone needs: the human equivalent of a cup of herbal tea.

## Stomaching (*n.*) *A cherishing of indignation or bitterness.*

I hadn't known that *stomach*, as a verb, meant both "to take offense at" and "to endure without complaint." But it does, and the first of these two senses has happily given rise to the malignant splendor of the word *stomaching*.

*also see:* ill-willy

**Storge** *(n.) Instinctive affection, especially such as parents have for their children.*

Surely no parent would tolerate his child's adolescence were it not for this inherent ability to like someone who is so often unlikable.

*also see:* antipelargy

**Subtrist** *(adj.) Slightly sad.*

I suppose there is really not much difference between this word and many others, such as *glum* or *melancholy*. But I like the way *subtrist* looks and sounds, and all the other Romance languages seem to have fashionable words like *triste*, which elegantly convey sadness with a Continental flair. Sometimes a word does not have to have a special meaning—it's enough simply to like its style.

*also see:* avidulous

**Superarrogate** *(v.) To act with tremendous arrogance.*

*Superarrogate* is interesting for two reasons—it describes arrogance of a superior order, and it functions as a verb, which *arrogant* by itself fails to do.

*also see:* testiculous

**Superchery** *(n.) Foul play; an attack made against one who is at a disadvantage.*

A twenty-five-cent word for a cheap shot.

*also see:* barla–fumble

# S

**Superfidel** *(adj.)* *Overly credulous; believing too much.*

Contrary to what one might reasonably believe, *superfidel* does not refer to a cigar-smoking communist superhero from Cuba. Though perhaps it could be applied to his followers.

*also see:* gobemouche

**Supersaliency** *(n.)* *"The leaping of the male for the act of copulation."* (OED)

Were this word to be used in a figurative sense it would seem perhaps immoderately effusive, and were it used literally it would seem to be potentially dangerous, so I'm not quite sure how it should be employed. But so singular a description as this must have a use somewhere, if only on Animal Planet.

*also see:* tripudiate

**Supervacaneous** *(adj.)* *Vainly added over and above what is needed.*

This word is in some way an example of itself, a redundant way of saying redundant, with a touch of vanity thrown in for good measure.

**Surfeited** *(adj.)* *Oppressed or disordered by eating too much.*

*Surfeited* lacks any of the pleasant connotations that are occasionally implied when someone finishes his meal and says "I'm stuffed." It simply means that you ate too much and now feel sick and dumb.

*also see:* obligurate, residentarian

**Swasivious** *(adj.) Persuasive in an agreeable fashion.*

The definition for *swasivious* would, on its face, seem a bit redundant. After all, I cannot think of a word to describe someone who is disagreeably persuasive.

**Sympatetic** *(n.) A companion one walks with.*

I found *sympatetic* hiding in the middle of a list of words under the prefix *sym-*. Discoveries like this one are what make reading the *OED* from cover to cover worthwhile.

LANGUAGES CHANGE. I HAVE KNOWN THIS for some time, but I did not fully appreciate how much and how rapidly our language changes until I began to read the *OED*.

For instance, I'd become so used to seeing the word *paraphernalia* with the word *drug* in front of it that I'd more or less assumed that the former had always been linked with the latter, and that it was probably of recent vintage, perhaps from the 1960s. However, it turns out that *paraphernalia* dates to at least the fifteenth century, and originally referred to the possessions of her own that a woman was allowed to keep when she entered into marriage. *Paraphernalia* doesn't even exist in the print edition of the *OED* in relation to drugs or drug use, although it has been included in the ongoing edit of the online version.

I snickered like my twelve-year-old self, looking up the dirty words in the dictionary, when I discovered that the original meaning of *fizzle* was to fart silently. It was the only meaning of *fizzle* for about three hundred years, beginning in the sixteenth century. And I found renewed appreciation for the word *docile*, which I'd assumed had always meant "easily cowed," when I found that its original meaning was "teachable."

I've discovered not only that words shift their meanings, or end up meaning something completely different; often it turns out that they are far older than I had thought, or far younger. *Ye olde*, that linguistic blister that afflicts the signs of so many touristy shops hawking prefabricated knickknacks made to look antique, apparently did not enter our language until the end of the nineteenth century. And its deformed cousin *shoppe* has its first written citation in 1933.

I was particularly surprised when I saw that *scumbag* (as used to describe an unpleasant person) entered the written language in 1971, not only because I thought the term had been introduced much earlier, but also because I have been assured by my parents that I was using this expression quite volubly and clearly in 1972, while still in diapers. Which means that either I was extremely up-to-date in my use of pejorative slang or extraordinarily profane at a young age—or both.

It was not terribly surprising to see that *disrespect* has existed as a noun since the early seventeenth century, but I had no idea that it was used as a verb even earlier. My impression was that "to disrespect" someone was African American urban slang from the

1980s, but I was off by at least a hundred years. And while I have my doubts as to whether there is a correlation between Spoonie Gee's use of *dis* in "Spoonin' Rap" circa 1980 ("Ya wanna be dissed and then ya wanna be a crook / Ya find a old lady, take her pocket-book") and George Meredith's use of *disrespect* in *Beauchamp's Career* circa 1876 ("Treating her . . . like a disrespected grand-mother"), I'd like to at least entertain the possibility that there is.

**Tacenda** (*n.*) *Things not to be mentioned; matters that are passed over in silence.*

> The incident with the broccoli. Your Aunt Tilly's first hus-band. Where that scar really came from.
> *also see:* nefandous

**Tacturiency** (*n.*) *The desire of touching.*

> The desire to touch something, rather than simply look at it, is probably responsible for more dissolved marriages than all other desires combined. Stick with *visuriency* (the desire of seeing).

**Tardiloquent** (*adj.*) *Talking slowly.*

> In my estimation, there are only two possible reasons people speak slowly. Either they are not quite bright enough to get the words out any faster or they think you aren't quite bright enough to understand them any other way. In either case

you're stuck in a conversation with someone who is *tardilo-quent*, and something has gone horribly wrong.

## Terriculament (*v.*) *To inspire one with groundless fear.*

Whether it's your parents telling you that your features will get stuck like that if you keep making that face or insurance companies telling you that a person your age dies every thirteen seconds, it seems like someone is always out there *terriculamenting* us.

*also see:* indread

## Testiculous (*adj.*) *Having large testicles.*

For this word the *OED* cites Nathan Bailey's dictionary of 1721, which memorably defines it as "that hath great cods." While it is clear what sense Bailey is using *cods*, it is not clear whether he intends *testiculous* to be used in a literal or figurative fashion. As a companion word of sorts, one could also employ the word *chalcenterous* (having bowels made of bronze; tough).

*also see:* superarrogate

## Thelyphthoric (*adj.*) *Morally corruptive or ruinous to women.*

When I was studying Latin in high school, we used to amuse ourselves by looking up the dirty words in the Latin-English dictionary. It was easy—they were the only entries for which the headword and definition both were provided in Latin, a means of protecting our impressionable young minds that was as subtle as an exclamation writ large that said, "Kids, do not look here." I don't really think the *OED* editors are doing the same thing here, but it's hard to be certain when they define a word in this way and then refuse to provide any specific examples of what they are talking about.

## Toe-cover (n.) *A present that is both useless and inexpensive.*

We all know that it's the thought that counts, but sometimes part of that thought should be not giving a useless present that you picked up at the corner store at the last minute.
*also see:* wonderclout

## Tricoteuse (n.) *A woman who knits; specifically, a woman who during the French Revolution would attend the guillotinings and knit while the heads were rolling.*

What I've learned from reading the *OED* has not been confined to vocabulary. I've also learned a good deal about the history of the unpleasantness of the human race, including the portrait of this unsympathetic character, the knitter who attends beheadings.

## Tripudiate (v.) *To dance, skip, or leap with excitement.*

Although I might have trouble dancing and skipping with joy (or admitting that I did), I would have no qualms about *tripudiating*, which somehow sounds a bit more dignified.
*also see:* supersaliency

**Trumpery** (*n.*) *"Something of less value than it seems."* (*Samuel Johnson,* A Dictionary of the English Language, *1755*)

Like your car.

*also see:* wonderclout

**Turkish** (*v.*) *To transform something, especially for the worse.*

I'd assumed that the *OED*, having been largely written in the nineteenth and early twentieth centuries, would be filled with all sorts of racist and otherwise offensive words. There are very few of them, however, and it is not clear whether this is due to the editors not wanting to offend or if they merely didn't think the words were qualified for inclusion. For instance, *frenchified* is listed, but without the sense that is given in a number of other dictionaries: "to be afflicted with a venereal disease."

**Twi-thought** (*n.*) *A vague or indistinct thought.*

My head is filled with *twi-thoughts* these days, and all are variations on a single theme: that word I've forgotten, the one flitting around somewhere in the back of my head, teasing my lips and not quite coming close enough to remember.

*also see:* velleity

# U

REACHING THE LETTER *U*, I feel for the first time that the end is in sight. I have decidedly mixed feelings about this, for along with these first glimmers of hope come the first glimmers of fear. What on earth will I read when I finish reading the *OED*? I still have thousands more pages to read, so I do not have to worry much yet about not having a book to read, and furthermore, I have to get through the massive lexicographic expanse that is *un-*.

When I told Alix that I was about to begin reading *un-* she groaned and said, "Oh, no, that's the biggest S-E section in the whole dictionary!" in a tone that made it sound like she was describing crossing a desert, not turning the pages of a book. "S-E," I soon learn, is lexicographic slang for "self-explanatory." Any *un-* word is judged to be self-explanatory if the *un-* modifies a word that is defined elsewhere in the dictionary and a reasonably conscientious reader can figure out its meaning. Apparently, when she'd worked for Merriam-Webster, Alix had had to define (or not define) all these words, and she recalled the experience with mixed emotions.

I soon realize why, as *un-* goes on for 451 pages, and reading a 451-page list composed largely of self-explanatory words is only slightly more exciting than reading the phone book.

After ten pages of this I think to myself, "This isn't so bad."

After twenty pages I begin entertaining thoughts of just skipping ahead to the end, reading the last *un-* word and pretending the whole thing never happened.

After fifty pages I sink deep into a petulant rage and turn the pages violently, occasionally tearing one, as though this whole enterprise was the invention of some cruel taskmaster other than myself.

By the time I've read one hundred pages I am near catatonic, bored out of my mind, and so listless I can't remember why wanted to read any of this in the first place. At this point, telling myself "You only have 351 more pages of *un-* words to go" does not seem helpful. I don't quite feel as though I have lost my mind, but it often seems as though it is on vacation somewhere else, just east of sanity.

I am convinced there must be some other use for this section of dictionary aside from it being an extraordinarily thorough scholarly record of some small corner of the alphabet. It could be used to lull unruly children to sleep or as an effective threat of punishment. It could be used to remove unwanted guests ("I would really love to read you some of my favorite pages from *un-*"). It could be used in much the same fashion that some convenience stores use Muzak, blasting it into their parking lots at night in order to repel idle teenagers.

But at certain points in the vast tundra of *un-*, in the midst of wondering why I don't just skip ahead and pretend I've read every word, I come across an entry so remarkably singular that it rouses me just enough to continue reading. Words such as *unbepissed* (which refers to something that has not been urinated on) and *underlive* (to live in a manner that does not measure up to one's potential).

Because it is at times such as this, under the duress of unrelenting tedium, that the true appeal of reading the dictionary makes itself known. It's not that I'm a great fan of boring activities, but they do make the rest of life that much more special when they come alive.

## Ultra-crepidarian (*n.*) *One who offers advice or criticism in matters beyond his scope; an ignorant or presumptuous critic.*

*Ultra-crepidarian* is a word born of a strange etymology. It comes from the Latin *ultra crepidam* (beyond the sole), which is itself a shortening of the response the ancient Greek painter Apelles famously gave to the shoemaker who had dared to repeatedly criticize his work.

## Umbriphilous (*adj.*) *Fond of the shade.*

Although this is a botanical word, used to describe things arboreal, I choose to use it to describe myself.

**Unasinous** *(adj.) Being equal to another in stupidity.*

If you are uncertain how one might use this word, just think of any two political parties.

*also see:* constult

**Unbepissed** *(adj.) Not having been urinated on; unwet with urine.*

Who ever thought there was an actual need for such a word? Is it possible that at some time there was such a profusion of things that *had* been urinated on that there was a pressing need to distinguish those that had not?

*also see:* lant

**Unconversable** *(adj.) Not suitable for social converse.*

The more time I spend reading the dictionary, the more *unconversable* I become. After a long day trying to wrestle obscure polysyllabic words into my brain I have difficulty engaging in any conversation beyond "make it a double."

**Undisonant** *(adj.) Making the sound of waves.*

The sound I believe is the most beautiful in the world, and the only conceivable reason to live in California.

*also see:* psithurism

**Unlove** *(v.) To cease loving a person.*

There is no easy way to tell someone that you no longer love them, and this rather obvious and blunt word does not offer even the slightest bit of euphemistic cover.

## Upchuck (*v.*) *To vomit.*

According to the *OED*'s citations for *upchuck*, the word was included in Harold Wentworth and Stuart Berg Flexner's magisterial *Dictionary of American Slang* (1960), which also supplied the additional information, "Considered a smart and sophisticated term c 1935, esp. when applied to sickness that had been induced by over-drinking." This is a classic example of language change: *upchuck* no longer has quite the same panache.

## Utinam (*n.*) *An earnest wish or yearning.*

*Utinam* is derived from a Latin word of the same spelling, which originally meant "oh, *that!*" Etymologies like this one make me doubt that languages are in fact formed in a logical rule-based fashion.

*also see:* desiderium

# V

ONE MORNING IN THE MIDST of this colossal project I woke up and, with mounting horror, realized that I actually knew the differences between Jacobean, Jacobian, Jacobin, and Jacobine. I did my utmost not to think about it, and the knowledge soon passed from my mind. But it is probably still lurking around in there somewhere, hiding in some dark corner, waiting for just the right inappropriate moment to jump out and ruin whatever conversation I might be having.

This got me wondering just how much useless information I've picked up through all this *OED* reading. A considerable amount, I would guess. I like to think that I'll forget it all soon, but I'm afraid that won't be the case. Some small part of my brain will be busying itself with holding on to all the words that are defined as "hiera picra" (nine) or all the different obscure words that begin with *g* and mean "to gnash the teeth" (*granch, grassil, grent, grint, grist,* and *gristbite*).

It might be a small part of my brain that is busying itself with these minutiae, but there's a lot of minutiae flowing in, and at some point it has to take a toll on how well my brain functions in other areas. Some part of my unconscious is forever occupied with trying to match a word with its definition or to remember what that funny etymology was. I imagine there are prefixes and suffixes forever becoming stuck, like bits of mud or grit, in the cogs of my memory. If I don't find a way to clear all this useless information out I'm afraid my critical faculties will seize up like a computer that has been asked to do too many things at once, and I'll forget how to speak altogether.

But is all this information really any more useless than much of the rest of the knowledge I've accumulated over the years? For example, at some point in the last thirty years I learned that Andrew Jackson's nickname was "Old Hickory" and that an earthworm experiences a rise in temperature of about one degree Fahrenheit for every three hundred feet it burrows into the ground. Are *granch, grassil,* and the rest of the teeth-gnashing words of any less value?

I have managed to willfully prevent one small bit of knowledge from entering my brain. Even though I now know that there are nine different words in the *OED* defined as "hiera picra," I have absolutely no idea what a hiera picra is. I'd already become tired of this definition by the time I reached *H*, and in a small and petty act of obstinacy I refused to read this one entry when I came across it. If you meet me at a cocktail party or in a library basement, please don't quiz me on it.

## Valentine (*v.*) *To greet with song at mating-time (said of birds).*

When birds open their mouths and let forth with song in the hopes of attracting a mate it falls into the category of "marvel of nature." When a man does this same activity it falls into the category of "grounds for a restraining order."

## Vanitarianism (*n.*) *The pursuing of vanities.*

Only one citation is provided for this word, and it comes, rather unsurprisingly, from Thackeray, a writer who seems to have an unreasoning fondness for the word *vanity*.

*also see:* quomodocunquize

## Velleity (*n.*) *A mere wish or desire for something without accompanying action or effort.*

Every once in a while I come across a word which years ago I misplaced and had long since forgotten. *Velleity* is one such word. Whenever I find a word like this it puts me in a good mood for several hours. It is as if I've just found money in my pocket that I'd forgotten was there.

*also see:* twi-thought

**Vicambulist** *(n.)* *One who walks about in the streets.*

Now that *streetwalker* has taken on connotations some people may not care to ascribe to themselves, we have a dearth of words to describe someone who simply likes to walk about in the streets of a city. Here's hoping *vicambulist* will enter everyday language anew.

*also see:* solivagant

**Videnda** *(n., pl.)* *Things worth seeing; things that ought to be seen.*

What every travel guidebook promises to capture and never actually does. Which must be why one so often sees them being sold in the dollar bin at used bookstores, or on window ledges, propping up air conditioners.

**Vitativeness** *(n.)* *The love of life.*

Let the French keep their *joie de vivre* and the Germans keep their *freude zu leben*, we have no need of these silly Continental expressions now. Actually, you're much more likely to get your point across if you use the expression *joie de vivre* than if you go with *vitativeness*, which seems to be a term used primarily by phrenologists in the nineteenth century.

**Vocabularian** *(n.)* *One who pays too much attention to words.*

In the past I have been accused by various parties of paying too much attention to words. Which is true, I suppose; but what else do I have to pay attention to?

# V

**Vomiturient** *(adj.) Characterized by a desire to vomit.*

For many people, *vomiturient* will conjure up images of hangovers, car rides, pregnancies, and other nauseating experiences. It makes me think of words such as *set* and prefixes such as *un-*, since if I have to read those passages again I will be feeling *vomiturient* indeed.

*compare:* nauseant

# W

SOMETHING IS A BIT OFF IN *W*. I was reading for a few hours before I remembered that there was no such letter in ancient Latin, and so the vocabulary of *W* is overwhelmingly Anglo-Saxon in origin. Some words from Greek and Latin roots have snuck in, usually in the form of compound words, but they are rare. The overall effect of this is fairly disconcerting—for more than twenty-thousand pages I'd been looking at a word list of which about 80 percent was derived from Greek and Latin, and suddenly it all changed. It was almost as if I had picked up the wrong dictionary.

The upside to this is that *W* has significantly fewer words of a scientific nature, which tend to be words I find achingly dull. The downside is that it also has fewer words that are fantastical or outrageous. Anglo-Saxon tends not to lend itself to long and elaborate words that have strung together three or four affixes to create a rhetorical term for a very obscure thing.

While reading all the way through a dictionary one notices things that one never would see if just browsing, or even if consistently looking up words. These things are generally not terribly interesting or useful, as when I read Alexander Warrack's Scottish dictionary and found that there were five or six different words all defined as "the viviparous blenny," which is not the term for the town drunk, but instead a type of small fish that bears its young live. I am perfectly content knowing just one or two words for the viviparous blenny, so I did not bother to write them all down.

But of the many things in the *OED* I have found striking, most tend to be considerably more interesting than varied descriptions of small fish. For instance, it has a tremendous number of words describing the state of being "deserving" or "worthy" of something. One can be deserving of derision (*irrisible*), of ruination (*perditionable*), or of receiving a beating (*verberable*). Something can be worthy of being rejected (*rejectaneous*), of being rejoiced at (*laetable*), or of being desired (*appetible*). One can be worthy of being helped (*helpworthy*) or a person who deserves to be whipped (*mastigoporer*).

If you've ever wondered whether there is a word for something, there is a fairly good chance that it does in fact exist, and the *OED* is the place to find it. I would encourage you to grab a volume and start looking. Even if you don't find the word you're hoping for, I promise you'll discover enough surprising and remarkable gems along the way to make up for any possible disappointment.

**Wailer** *(n.) A professional mourner; one who is paid to weep.*

What does it say about us, as speakers of this language, that we have need for any word that denotes a hired mourner at a funeral, much less the fact that there was apparently enough demand for such services that we've managed to accumulate at least a half dozen terms for it? In addition to *wailer*, we have *black, keener, moirologist, mute,* and *weeper,* all of which of the *OED* reveals as one who is paid to mourn.

**Well-aired** *(adj.) Having sweet-smelling breath.*

I think we can all agree that this is a wishful, mythical quality. With breath, as with family reunions, the most that one can reasonably hope for is an absence of bad.

**Well-corned** *(adj.) Exhilarated or excited with liquor.*

Happy-drunk, as opposed to *barley-hood* (drunk and mean). *also see:* perpotation

**Well-lost** *(adj.) Lost in a good cause or for a good consideration.*

As in the lie ("I'm helping to fund public education") people tell themselves when they fail to win the lottery for the ten-thousandth time.

## Well-woulder *(n.) A conditional well-wisher.*

The *well-woulder* is far more common than the everyday well-wisher; he may in some small way wish you success, just so long as it is not more success than he has.

*also see:* backfriend

## Wine-knight *(n.) A person who drinks valiantly.*

As entries occasionally are in the *OED*, this is wonderfully unclear. How exactly does one drink valiantly? Draw your own conclusions.

## Wonderclout *(n.) A thing that is showy but worthless.*

Surgically augmented breasts and a large vocabulary are two things that come to mind when I contemplate that which is showy and of little value, but I'm certain that you can think of others.

*also see:* toe-cover, trumpery

# X

AN ENTREATY: STOP THINKING ABOUT the dictionary as though it is nothing more than a cold and foreboding authority—a finger-shaking, tsk-tsking book that only exists to tell you that you are wrong about something. Stop viewing it as the book that is consulted only in times of linguistic duress. Stop putting it away after you've looked something up; instead, leave it out, and start reading it.

The previous chapters, chronicling as they do my loss of eyesight, sanity, and social graces, might not be seen as an effective exhortation to go out and read the dictionary, but this is exactly what I am proposing. Just go get a dictionary and read it.

You do not have to read the whole thing. You could start with the *OED*, and tackle just one letter—*X*, for instance. It forms by far the shortest section in the *OED*, only thirteen pages, short enough to read in an evening. Make yourself a nightcap, a warm cup of milk, or whatever drink suits your fancy, sit down in the most comfortable armchair in the house, and read *X*. It might not be the most interesting letter in the alphabet, but you can read it all the way through, and once you have you can say to yourself that you've read absolutely everything the *OED* has to say about words that begin with the letter *x*.

Or you could start smaller than a whole letter—you could just find a prefix you like, and leave a bookmark in it. *Be-* is a fine prefix to walk through, as are *for-* and *ob-*. Leave the dictionary sitting out, and let your eyes light on it whenever you happen by.

The dictionary you set out to read does not have to be some massive and unabridged multivolume work, nor does it have to be particularly current. If you are looking for up-to-date information on our language, you shouldn't be looking at a reference book from the nineteenth or early twentieth century. However, if you are simply looking to be educated in unexpected ways by a book, you can readily accomplish this with any one of a number of outdated dictionaries.

Find a good college dictionary, like any of the eleven Merriam-Webster has published. (I myself am partial to the tenth edition, but that is mainly because it's the one Alix worked on.) We have eight or nine of them lying around the house, and so one is always within reach. We need only take a step out of the kitchen or lean forward on the couch to find a word. Do not think that just because it is called a collegiate dictionary and you yourself have already graduated from college, it is somehow beneath you or you wouldn't learn much from it. You will make discoveries on every page; even if they're only minor discoveries, you'll be pleased to have stumbled upon them.

How many books can you think of that have such an abundance of useful information? How many authors say something interesting on every single page? Reading the dictionary reminds me of the first time I read Gabriel García Márquez—I was astounded that any writer could capture my interest so unrelentingly.

I suppose it is possible that many readers will consider me touched in the head for suggesting this. But for those of you who are willing and able to begin viewing dictionaries as something other than the embodiment of that scolding English teacher, the one who tortured you over your creatively spelled words and dubious syntax, go ahead—grab any dictionary and start reading it.

Well, perhaps not any dictionary; there are a great number of bad dictionaries out there.

For instance, hundreds of "Webster's" dictionaries have been published in the last 150 years. Shortly after George and Charles Merriam bought the rights to publish Noah Webster's dictionary in 1844 they displayed what was either a serious lack of knowledge regarding copyright law or an almost touchingly naïve faith in their fellow publishers to not infringe on their property. When the copyright lapsed they suddenly found themselves in direct competition with an enormous number of other "Webster's" dictionaries, put out by anyone who had access to some sort of word list and the means of printing a book. Lawsuits were filed, but it was too late—the name "Webster" had gone the way of the Hoover, and was public domain and free for any publisher to use as the name of a dictionary.

Most of the major American dictionary publishers today put out some form of dictionary they call "Webster's," and some of them are quite good. However, back in the late nineteenth and early twentieth centuries an enormous number of what could charitably be called fake Webster's were floating around. My favorite one is a small volume from 1940 that was promulgated (I don't want to say *published*) by the Standard Oil Company. It appears to have been intended to be either sold or given away for free at gas stations. This is not the kind of dictionary one should read.

Stay away from grade school dictionaries, dictionaries for students learning English as a second language, and encyclopedic dictionaries that are full of extraneous information like a list of all the past vice presidents of the United States or the average rainfall in Bolivia. Do not buy any dictionary that has been printed on newsprint.

*Funk and Wagnalls* dictionaries are great, and so are *Century* dictionaries. Nose around in a used bookstore and you'll almost certainly find a nice old *Random House* or a decent *Thorndike Barnhart*.

Or just get yourself a set of the *OED*. It takes up less room than a television set and is infinitely more useful. Start looking up words for which you already know the meaning, and read how these words have been used over the ages. Start troving for words you've never heard of, one at a time. Start reading about words that you'll never need to know, just because sometimes it's nice to know something superfluous.

And don't be surprised if you find that once you start leafing through the pages of this dictionary it suddenly grabs hold and it is unclear whether it is the book that won't let go of you, or you who won't let go of the book.

## Xanthodontous *(adj.) Having teeth that are yellow, as do some rodents.*

If you are referring to someone as having yellow teeth, the chances that you are paying him or her a compliment seem pretty slim, so you might as well get more bang for your buck and use this fine word, which also implies the person shares other rodentlike characteristics.

## Xenium *(n.) A gift given to a guest.*

It is a very delicate balance to strike, this business of giving a gift to someone you do not want to offend and yet whom you also do not want to encourage to stick around too long. Unless you are one of those unbalanced individuals who actually enjoys having company, I would recommend giving a *xenium* such as a pair of used socks, something that says "Here is a gift—please go away."

**Xenogenesis** (*n.*) *Offspring that does not resemble its parents.*

The reason God invented paternity suits.

*also see:* killcrop

**Xerostomia** (*n.*) *A dryness of the mouth caused by insufficient production of saliva.*

A word that makes my mouth dry just thinking of it. Very few people go around thinking to themselves, "I wish I had a lot more spit in my mouth," which is probably why you've never heard of this condition.

Much about the English language we seem to find impossible to agree on. Can we use *hopefully* as a sentential adverb, is *irregardless* a word or not, and is it finally okay to go ahead and split that damn infinitive? In some ways these ongoing arguments are not terribly surprising—people like to feel that they are an authority on something, and they like to argue—and if you set your mind to it you can continue arguing in a semiauthoritative way about these aspects of the language for a very long time. But on a deeper level we also find it difficult to get people to agree on even some basic quantitative aspects of English—such as how many words are in it, or how many words the average person knows.

The general view of how many words are in the English language ranges from several hundred thousand to several million. If scientific terminology is included, the number swells to several million. If you add or exclude archaic words, or slang terms, the number goes up or down accordingly. Given that there is no real way of getting everyone to agree on what the parameters are for such a word count, there can be no way to agree on how many of them we have.

Similarly, there is no real consensus on how many words an average speaker of the English language knows. Rather than trying to ratchet up my personal word count and fancify my vocabulary for cocktail parties, I read the *OED* so that I might know what the words are for the things in the world that I had always thought to be unnamed. And perhaps if I know there is a word for something (such as the smell of newly fallen rain) I will stop and pay more attention to it.

If you have occasion and reason to use these words, so much the better. But even if you do not, there should be no reason why you cannot carry them with you and enjoy them nonetheless.

## Yepsen (*n.*) *The amount that can be held in two hands cupped together; also, the two cupped hands themselves.*

A measurement that has never really caught on like the teaspoon, the *yepsen* also falls firmly within the category of things for which you never thought there was a word—at least, not until some interfering busybody like me came along and told you what it was.

**Yesterneve** (*n.*) *Yesterday evening.*

There are a number of words for describing time, well beyond simply saying today, tomorrow, or yesterday.

Hesternal—*of or relating to yesterday.*

Nudiustertian—*of or relating to the day before yesterday.*

Overmorrow—*of or relating to the day after tomorrow.*

Postriduan—*done on the following day.*

Yestermorn—*yesterday morning.*

**Yuky** (*adj.*) *Itchy; also, itching with curiosity.*

A Scottish and northern English dialectical word with a world of applications.

# Z

I USED TO ENJOY FISHING. But I hated catching fish, so I would take great care to ensure this wouldn't occur, by baiting the hook with nothing and fishing in places where I was fairly certain I would have no accidental success. My reasoning was that sitting on a dock or a riverbank, smelling the water and listening to its sounds, was a perfectly splendid way to spend a few hours—why would I want to ruin it by hooking and reeling in a fish?

In its own peculiar way, the *OED* has been my fishing pole, the means by which I while away a great deal of time in seclusion and accomplish nothing concrete. I have no intention of using these words I have found; their enjoyment comes primarily from simply finding them and recognizing that they exist.

I have been trying to not think about it, but once I begin to read *Z*, it becomes inescapably clear that the end of my project is fast approaching. I've spent months and months curled up in the corner of this room, shut away from sunlight, society, and all other such irritants. Soon I will not have the excuse of reading to fall back on. The thought that greets me every morning now as I approach the end of this twentieth volume of the *OED* is "What will I read next?" This is followed by a curious mixture of elation and depression.

In an attempt to forestall the gloom, I've been thinking about what things I've learned from reading it. I am not thinking so much of what specific bits of information I've managed to retain, but rather about the life lessons that this yearlong experience has given me. The list I began to form is not terribly encouraging.

I did not wear glasses when I began reading the *OED*. Over the course of the past year my eyesight has deteriorated significantly, and the only benefit I can see in this is that it makes my physical decline in other areas seem minor in comparison. My back hurts much more than when I was a furniture mover, and my neck will periodically seize up with a blossoming pain. I've not been crippled by reading, but I'm certainly not as fit as I was before I spent twelve months confined to a chair.

I've also become seized with the fear that the words I use, either in speech or writing, actually mean something different from what I think they do, or have a secondary or tertiary meaning that I do not intend to express. I now spend an inordinate amount of time checking and rechecking the words I use. This would be perfectly acceptable were I in the process of writing a dissertation or a formal letter, but when I do it while writing a grocery list or a note to Alix to remind her of something it seems a bit silly. I also speak considerably more slowly, either because I'm looking for just the right word (that I now know exists somewhere out there in my memory) or because I am easily confused by all the newfound choices I have.

I have a greatly increased tolerance for coffee. I've always been a coffee drinker, but I've never had the time, inclination, or need to truly devote myself to it the way I have over the past year. I am uncertain whether or not this is a benefit. On the one hand, it has brought me comfort and pleasure. On the other hand, my teeth are browning rapidly.

In a more positive vein, I've also learned that any headache, no matter how severe it is, will eventually go away. I've learned that I will not lose my mind if I do nothing but sit in a chair ten hours a day, for an entire year. I've learned that no matter how large a book is, if I just keep reading sooner or later I will finish it.

I've gained a renewed appreciation for just how glorious the English language can be. I have a greater respect for lexicographers in general, and for the ones who worked on the *OED* in particular. I've gained a much greater understanding of how much I do not know.

I've also fulfilled a wish from childhood: to spend my days simply reading. I've often wondered what it would be like to have nothing else to do—would the activity lose its appeal and become in some way tainted by its quotidian drudgery? For me it has not.

I wish I could paint a picture of this experience as more of a struggle, one that threatened to land me in an insane asylum, or poised to jump off a bridge, the pages of the dictionary fluttering in my wake as I hurtled toward the menacing water. The truth is: it has been downright enjoyable.

### Zabernism (n.) *The misuse of military authority; bullying or aggression.*

According to the *OED*, this eternally germane word comes from an unfortunate episode that occurred in 1912, in the village of Zabern, in Alsace, during which a German officer purportedly shot a cobbler who smiled at him. Which pretty much brings us to the world today.

### Zoilus (n.) *An envious critic.*

Taken from the name of a Greek critic (fourth century BCE) who had a tremendous dislike for Homer. Saint Augustine also disliked reading Homer, but he at least had the excuse of finding the Greek language difficult. Critics, beware: you're of course entitled to your opinions, but if fate turns its back on you, your name might be forever linked with the notion of a carping and pathetic nitpicker.

### Zugzwang (n.) *A disagreeable position in which a chess player is obliged to move but cannot do so without disadvantage.*

*Zugzwang* is a chess term, but it would seem to have wide applicability in everyday life. In fact, it seems odd that there's no other word for this. Such are the surprises of the *OED*: there was enough need to coin a word like *unbepissed*, but not one to describe the fairly common experience of being in an untenable position and needing to make a decision.

*also see:* pessimum

# Zyxt (*v.*) *To see.*

There is nothing terribly interesting about *zyxt*. It is the second-person singular indicative present form of the verb "to see" in the Kentish dialect and has obviously not been in common use for some time. Given that in the new online edition it has been stripped of its headword status and moved to the middle of a heap of variant spellings of *see*, it seems unlikely that it will ever return to vogue. I do not think I will ever use it in conversation, and it is highly doubtful I will ever hear it used. However, it will always be a word I remember fondly, as it is the very last word defined in the *Oxford English Dictionary*.

# Excursus
## (Bibliography)

I FINISHED READING THE *OED* at 2:17 p.m. on July 18, 2007. My initial reaction was incredulity mixed with glee, followed by a surprising sense of accomplishment. Why was this surprising? Because I still felt that I did not actually do anything concrete. All I did was sit down and read for a year, admittedly in a fairly persistent and ferocious fashion. Whether deserved or not, I got up and danced a small jig of triumph, startling some mice who had been creeping toward the sandwich in my backpack.

After I finished dancing my jig I sat there and debated whether or not I want to read the bibliography. I told myself that it is not really part of the dictionary, and that furthermore, I'd already read all the names of the authors and their books as I went through the dictionary. And it is only a partial bibliography. That night over dinner I told Alix that I was finished reading. She asked, "How was the bibliography?"

217

I replied in as offhand a way as I could manage that I'd decided not to read it. She gave me that steady look that is so quietly indicative of disapproval and after a moment said, "You are going to say that you read the whole *OED* and you are not going to read the bibliography?" The next day I began reading again.

Immediately I realized that I should have read the bibliography before reading *Z*, as this was not quite the exultant and dramatic manner of finishing this project that I had envisioned. It is almost impossible to read, dull on such a monumental level that I had immense trouble getting through even a few pages at a time. The bibliography has no overt personality. It was about as exciting as reading the family tree of someone you do not know or care about at all.

The bibliography has no definitions to marvel at, no etymologies to leave me scratching my head in either wonderment or bafflement, no occasional editorial clucking to make me laugh. It contains none of the sparkle or wit, or the temperamental oddities, that make up the previous twenty-one-thousand–odd pages. It is really nothing but a mildly interesting and very long list, and the more I tried to read through it the more it became clear that there was indeed only one important conclusion it could impart to me.

I missed reading the *OED*.

This was certainly not the conclusion I had expected. I'd thought that perhaps I would fling down the twentieth volume with a whoop and run off to bury myself in a month's worth of airport novels (or railway novels, as their nineteenth-century critics called them).

# Excursus

I had not planned for this. In fact, as I read through I put together a far greater list of words than the one I have included in this book. I wrote down all the words that end in -ee and -ix. I kept tabs on all the words that mean "hiding in a corner" or "full of sand." I wrote down every word I wished I'd known at some point in the past or hoped that I'd have occasion to want to know in the future. And as I wrote them all down, I thought to myself, "Now I will never have to read the *OED* again." This, of course, was absurd. I didn't *have* to read the *OED* in the first place; I read it because I wanted to, and furthermore, I had a wonderful time doing so. It was the most engrossing and enjoyable book I've ever read.

I miss waking up every morning before my alarm goes off, so excited to get up and begin reading that even in sleep I could not stop thinking about words. I miss finding answers to questions that I've had for years, and then forgetting the answers, and then finding them again. I miss the reading headaches. I miss the growing sense of excitement that arises from reading through a prefix, a letter, an alphabet; the excitement that grows as the pages remaining diminish. I miss coming up to the end of each volume.

And that's the problem—I've already read it, and I know how the story ends.

So I find myself faced with the question of what to read next. Should I try to learn Dutch so that I might begin reading through the forty-odd–volume dictionary they're working on in the Netherlands? I'm not terribly interested in this. Should I read the *New York Times* from its inception to the present, or begin reading phone books? This likewise does not resonate with me: as absurd as it was to read the *OED*, it was still an absurdity with a purpose, and not just reading for reading's sake.

There is really only one book I can think of that I have an enormous and palpable desire to read, and it is the one I just finished. I'm aware some people might think that the only thing more odd than reading the *OED* is to read it twice, and if this is so then I will be quite happily odd.

I've decided I will start reading again, and I'll start at *A*. But this time I'll be reading with no deadline. Anytime I come across something that catches my interest I will allow myself the leisure to stop and go investigate it for as long as I like. When I see a word I remember as being defined differently elsewhere, I'll go over to my other dictionaries and spend the rest of the day looking through them. When I get a headache I'll go take a walk and come back to the dictionary later in the evening. I'll listen to music while I read, and if the music is too distracting I'll pause in the reading and listen to the music until the words on the page in front of me beckon and become themselves too distracting to focus on the music.

So much of my life to date has been defined by reading books, and then looking for more books to read once I've finished. And in an epiphanic sort of way I've now realized that all the books I've read before have been but a preamble to this one glorious book I've just finished.

As I read through it again I will dawdle and browse, skip ahead and back, and perhaps even put it down every once in a while. The *OED* serves as a conduit to almost the entirety of great literature, and to a sizable portion of not-so-great literature as well. When I find a citation from Shakespeare or Urquhart that piques my fancy I might momentarily put the *OED* back on the shelf and go off to read the book cited. But it is more likely I will not do this, and instead will admire that citation from afar, from within the doorway of my dictionary.

It is only after I finished reading the *OED* that I fully realized why I had begun the project in the first place. I had hoped that within its pages I would find everything I had ever looked for in a novel: joy and sorrow, laughter and frustration, and the excitement and contentment that is unique to great storytelling. The *OED* exceeded all of these hopes and expectations. It is the greatest story I've ever read.

# Post-Excursus

WHEN PEOPLE DISCOVER THAT I took a year of my life to read the *Oxford English Dictionary* from beginning to end, they usually ask a fairly predictable series of questions. The first of these is almost inevitably "Why?" This is followed by "Are you mad?" or some variation thereof. Those who aren't able to gracefully extricate themselves from the conversation often then ask, "What will you read next?" a query that is followed by suggestions of other long non-narrative texts that I might engorge my head with, such as the telephone book.

This reaction saddens me. Is reading the dictionary really the literary equivalent of reading the phone book? I can well understand that many, or most, people would have neither the time nor the inclination to read an entire dictionary, but I find it regrettable that so many readers seem surprised that the experience is not just arduous or even informative but transporting.

I've met a number of people who happily confess that they read railroad timetables. On the face of it this might seem to be even less literary than reading the dictionary. But when you look just slightly past the black and white of the text, over-whelmingly made up of numerals and place names, there is something else within. Time and again I've heard these sched-ule readers tell me that they visit places through such reading, replaying the memories of where they've traveled in the past, and imagining the places where they would like to go in the future.

A railroad timetable now strikes me as a delightful thing to read. When I was young, my parents would try to impress upon me that spending time watching television was of less value than time spent reading, because it took no imagination to simply stare at a small glass screen of moving pictures. Reading a book, how-ever, required an imaginative effort. If this is true, wouldn't it also be true that reading a schedule of where and when the trains go (and constructing entire narratives, remembrances, and dreams from these minimalist symbols) requires an even greater burst of imagination than reading a novel?

So the answer to the question of why I decided to read this mammoth dictionary is that it is as transporting and literary as I allow it to be. As to the second question, I will plead emphatically guilty to madness, but only in the fourth sense of that word as it is defined in the *OED*, "Extravagant excitement or enthusiasm; ecstasy." For the query of what I will read next I have already answered it in the chapter before this one—I will continue to read this dictionary. But there are a plethora of other things I now want to read as well.

Because in addition to those who question my reasons and sanity for reading dictionaries, I have also met a smaller number of like-minded readers of books that are not driven inexorably by plot or dialogue. There are the aforementioned readers of rail-road timetables, and readers of other dictionaries. I met a man who told me that every morning for the past several decades he has started his day by taking a bath while reading from one of the sixty volumes of the *Oxford Dictionary of National Biography*. I've met a large number of people who read antique mail-order catalogs—which are essentially lists of items that once were for sale but no longer are. In every instance, these readers have com-mented on how captivated they were by the literary quality of what they were reading. I've not yet met anyone who reads phone books, but perhaps such people exist; people who can spend an entire day in a comfortable armchair, running their finger down the lines of similarly named families and the attendant phone numbers, perhaps constructing elaborate narratives around each one.

And why not? Any of these things—whether it is a word's defi-nition, a telephone number's designation, the description of an article of clothing, or the destination of a train—has the ability to draw from us emotion and memory far beyond what we might expect.

If what we are reading evokes wonder, sadness, and joy; if it makes us stay up later and get up earlier than we'd planned; if it leads us to reject the company of others while at the same time making us feel more a part of humanity—if what we are reading can do all these things, then how can we deny that what we're reading is a great book?

In the spirit of continued *OED* exploration, I've gathered a few words that didn't make it into the hardcover edition of this book. For those interested in continuing the journey with me, please read on.

## Anatiferous—(*adj.*) *Producing geese or ducks.*

I have often said that I never come away from reading the dictionary feeling stupider than when I began. This does not mean that I haven't occasionally come away feeling more confused. The entry for *anatiferous* does mention that barnacles were formerly thought to grow on trees, and, after they fell into the water were know as "tree-geese," but somehow this does not make me feel that I have a greater understanding of *anatiferous*, barnacles, or waterfowl.

## Bacony—(*adj.*) *In a state of fatty degeneration.*

How sad it is, at least for pigs, that this word never gained the traction of, or even replaced, the word *obese*.

## Bestink—(*v.*) *To afflict with stink.*

I think it's high time we have at our disposal a word, related to stinkiness, that carries with it the eternal truth that smelling bad rarely occurs in a social vacuum. So before you daub yourself in foul perfume, or decide to once more eschew the shower, think a bit on the word *bestink*.

## Bulbitate—(v.) *"To befilth one's breech."* (*Cockeram 1623*)

It seems to me that befilthing one's breeches is quite possibly the least dignified part of one's day. So it is only fitting that, as compensation, that we should have such a dignified-sounding word with which to describe it.

## Catillate—(v.) *"To licke dishes."* (*Cockeram 1623*)

*Catillate* is yet another one of the many words that Henry Cockeram made up for his dictionary. It is somewhat odd in that most words having to do with licking kitchen items (*lick-dish*, *lick-spigot*, and the like) seem to connote parasites, a quality *catillate* appears to have avoided.

## Crump—(v.) *Making the sound of feet crushing slightly frozen snow.*

Crump has many meanings, and almost all of them are sad, violent, or just downright unpleasant. It can mean a professional perjurer or an explosion; it can describe the crookedness of an old man's limbs or the act of bombarding with heavy artillery. Perhaps it is because it is assigned so many unhappy meanings that *crump* also enjoys such a delightful definition as the sound of crunching snow.

**Dactylodeiktous** *(adj.)—Pointed at with a finger.*
This is the perfect word for those of you who struggle through life tortured by the suspicion that you are missing out on substituting some unnecessarily complicated word for a very common occurrence.

**Emunction**—*(n.) The action of wiping the nose.*
*Emunction* is a sort of delicate lace handkerchief of a word, lending a degree of refinement to an otherwise indelicate act.

**Pick-mote**—*(n.) A person who points out trivial faults in others.*
Too often, when confronted with such a creature, we are forced to rely on such non-pejorative words and expressions as *den mother* and *nudger*. But these people deserve their very own specific bit of opprobrium, and *pick-mote* fits the bill quite nicely.

**Satisdiction**—*(n.) Saying enough.*
The rare case of a word that is the perfect example of itself.

**Scringe**—*(v.) To shrug the back or shoulders from cold.*
Discovering this word in the middle of a New York winter has enabled me to take note of two truths that I likely would not have noticed quite so much in more clement weather: (1) I scringe often from December through March, and (2) knowing what to call this bit of bad posture doesn't make it any less unpleasant.

**Unairable**—(*adj.*) *Incapable of forming good music.*

Some things are so common that we can't imagine not knowing what to call them. So how is it that we manage to live in a world surrounded by horrible music and have gotten by without this word?

**Vulpeculated**—(*pa. pple.*) *Robbed by a fox.*

I sincerely doubt that anyone reading this will ever be robbed by a fox. In fact, is seems almost certain that devoting any memory and effort at all to this word would unquestionably be a waste of time. But one of the great rewards of reading the *OED*, and familiarizing oneself with its more obscure and outdated words, is that it is one of the few of life's endeavors that can leave you feeling like you've bettered yourself, when in fact you've been a wastrel.

# Further Reading

PROBABLY NO BOOK HAS DONE so much in recent times to introduce the *OED* to the general public as has Simon Winchester's *The Professor and the Madman*. In addition, he is the author of *The Meaning of Everything*, which is a more detailed history of the *OED*, but no less entertaining than its predecessor.

If you are interested in finding out more about the *OED*, these and a number of other books are easily available and well worth looking at. Oxford University Press publishes *A Guide to the Oxford English Dictionary*, by Donna Lee Berg, an incredibly informative user's guide.

For those who are more inclined toward the historical, I would recommend *Caught in the Web of Words: James Murray and the Oxford English Dictionary*, a history of the dictionary and a biography of the man most responsible for it, written by his

# Further Reading

granddaughter, K. M. Elisabeth Murray. It is indispensable for anyone who wishes to know more about the creation of this dictionary.

For those who are interested in a history of the dictionary in a somewhat different vein, there is Lynda Mugglestone's *Lost for Words: The Hidden History of the Oxford English Dictionary*. It is an account of the making of the dictionary based on the edited proofs, and it is one of the most fascinating books I have ever read. Mugglestone is a wonderful scholar whose prose is no less readable for her erudition. She is also the editor of a collection of essays about the dictionary, titled *Lexicography and the OED: Pioneers in the Untrodden Forest*.

And, of course, there is always the *OED* itself.

# PENGUIN REFERENCE

**THE MEANING OF TINGO**
ADAM JACOT DE BOINOD

Did you know that the Albanians have twenty-seven words for moustache?

Or that in Hungary pigs go röf-röf-röf?

Or that tingo is an Easter Island word meaning 'to borrow things from a friend's house one by one until there's nothing left'?

Here are the most weird and wonderful words from all around the world, showing the curious ways different countries talk about food, emotions, animals and even facial hair – as well as many things you hadn't even realized had words to describe them …

'A book no well-stocked bookshelf, cistern-top or handbag should be without' Stephen Fry

'A luscious list of linguistic one-liners' *Daily Express*

# PENGUIN LANGUAGE

## TOUJOURS TINGO
## ADAM JACOT DE BOINOD

*The Meaning of Tingo*, Adam Jacot de Boinod's bestselling collection of bizarre and brilliant words from around the world, was acclaimed as:

'Absolutely delicious' Stephen Fry

'A luscious list of linguistic one-liners' *Daily Express*

'Very funny' *Independent on Sunday*

Now he's back with far more, from **gwarlingo** (Welsh – the rushing sound a grandfather clock makes before striking the hour) to **magimiks belong Yesus** (Tok Pisin – a helicopter) to **Tantenverführer** (German – a young man with suspiciously good manners). Oh, and Tingo is an Easter Island word meaning to borrow objects from a friend's house one by one until there are none left ...

Drawing on the collective wisdom of over 300 languages, *Toujours Tingo* has discovered all kinds of actions and objects, tastes and noises that English simply doesn't have the vocabulary for. We've all met a **layogenic** (Tagalog – a person who is only good-looking from a distance), a **jayus** (Indonesian – someone who tells a joke so unfunny that you can't help laughing), and even a **mouton enragé** (French – someone usually calm who loses their temper).

So whether you are **physiggoomai** (Ancient Greek – excited by eating garlic) or **knedlikovy** (Czech – rather partial to dumplings), there are riches here to charm and amuse everyone ...

# PENGUIN REFERENCE

## THE WONDER OF WHIFFLING
ADAM JACOT DE BOINOD

*The Meaning of Tingo* was a global smash hit: now Adam Jacot de Boinod uncovers the extraordinary words of his own English language.

*The Wonder of Whiffling* is a hugely enjoyable, surprising and rewarding tour of English around the globe (with fine coinages from our English-speaking cousins across the pond, Down Under and elsewhere). Discover all sorts of words you've always wished existed but never knew, such as *fornale*, to spend one's money before it has been earned; *cagg*, a solemn vow or resolution not to get drunk for a certain time; and *petrichor*, the pleasant smell that accompanies the first rain after a dry spell.

Delving passionately into the English language, Adam Jacot de Boinod also discovers why it is you wouldn't want to have dinner with a vice admiral of the narrow seas, why Jacobites toasted the little gentleman in black velvet, and why a Nottingham Goodnight is better than one from anywhere else.

'You'll never be lost for words again. Truly enlightening!' Mariella Frostrup

# PENGUIN SCIENCE

### THE BLANK SLATE STEVEN PINKER

'The best book on human nature that I or anyone else will ever read. Truly magnificent' Matt Ridley, *Sunday Telegraph*

'A passionate defence of the enduring power of human nature ... both life-affirming and deeply satisfying' Tim Lott, *Daily Telegraph*

'Brilliant ... enjoyable, informative, clear, humane' *New Scientist*

'If you think the nature/nurture debate has been resolved, you are wrong. It is about to be reignited with a vengeance ... this book is required reading' *Literary Review*

'Startling ... Pinker makes his main argument persuasively and with great verve ... This is a breath of air for a topic that has been politicized for too long' *Economist*

### HOW THE MIND WORKS STEVEN PINKER

'Why do memories fade? Why do we lose our tempers? Why do fools fall in love? Pinker's objective in this erudite account is to explore the nature and history of the human mind' *Sunday Times*

'Witty popular science that you enjoy reading for the writing as well as for the science' *The New York Review of Books*

### THE LANGUAGE INSTINCT STEVEN PINKER

'A marvellously readable book...illuminates every facet of human language: its biological origin, its uniqueness to humanity, its acquisition by children, its grammatical structure, the production and perception of speech, the pathology of language disorders and its unstoppable evolution' *Nature*

'An extremely valuable book, informative and well written' Noam Chomsky

'Brilliant ... Pinker describes every aspect of language, from the resolution of ambiguity to the way speech evolved ... he expounds difficult ideas with clarity, wit and polish' Stuart Sutherland, *Observer*

# PENGUIN SCIENCE

---

**THE STUFF OF THOUGHT:**
**LANGUAGE AS A WINDOW INTO HUMAN NATURE**
STEVEN PINKER

'Moments of genuine revelation and some very good jokes'
Mark Haddon, *Sunday Telegraph*

*The Stuff of Thought* is an exhilarating work of non-fiction. Surprising, thought-provoking and incredibly enjoyable, there is no other book like it – Steven Pinker will revolutionise the way you think about language. He analyses what words actually mean and how we use them, and he reveals what this can tell us about ourselves. He shows how we use space and motion as metaphors for more abstract ideas, and uncovers the deeper structures of human thought that have been shaped by evolutionary history. He also explores the emotional impact of language, from names to swear words, and shows us the full power that it can have over us. And, with this book, he also shows just how stimulating and entertaining language can be.

'Astonishingly readable' *Daily Telegraph*

'Perceptive, amusing and intelligent' *The Times*

'No one writes about language as clearly as Steven Pinker, and this is his best book yet' *Financial Times*

---

# PENGUIN WRITERS' GUIDES

**HOW TO PUNCTUATE**
GEORGE DAVIDSON

**HOW TO WRITE BETTER ENGLISH**
ROBERT ALLEN

**HOW TO WRITE EFFECTIVE EMAILS**
R. L. TRASK

**IMPROVE YOUR SPELLING**
GEORGE DAVIDSON

**WRITING FOR BUSINESS**
CHRIS SHEVLIN

The Penguin Writers' Guides series provides authoritative, succinct and easy-to-follow guidance on specific aspects of written English. Whether you need to brush up your skills or get to grips with something for the first time, these invaluable guides will help you find the best way to communicate clearly and effectively.

**Get your message across**

# PENGUIN LANGUAGE

**THE STORIES OF ENGLISH**
DAVID CRYSTAL

How did a language originally spoken by a few thousand Anglo-Saxons become one used by more than 1,500 million people? How have all the different versions of English evolved and changed? In this compelling global tour, David Crystal turns the traditional view of the history of the language on its head and tells the *real* stories of English that have never before been fully told.

'A spirited celebration . . . Crystal gives the story of English a new plot' *Guardian*

'Rejoices in dialects, argots and cants . . . enlightening – in a word, excellent' *Sunday Times*

'An exhilarating read . . . Crystal is a sort of latter-day Johnson' *The Times Higher Education Supplement*

'*The Stories of English* reads like an adventure story. Which, of course, it is' Roger McGough

'A marvellous book . . . for anyone who loves the English language(s) it will be a treasure-house' Philip Pullman

# PENGUIN REFERENCE

**THE LORE OF THE LAND**
WESTWOOD AND SIMPSON

> Where can you find the 'Devil's footprints'?
>
> What happened at the 'hangman's stone'?
>
> Did Sweeney Todd, the demon barber of Fleet Street, really exist?
>
> Where was King Arthur laid to rest?

Bringing together tales of hauntings, highwaymen, family curses and lovers' leaps, this magnificent guide will take you on a magical journey through England's legendary past.

'A real treasury' Philip Pullman

'A treasure-house of extraordinary tales, rooted in the wildly various and haunted landscapes of England' *Sunday Times*

'A fascinating county-by county guidebook to headless horsemen, bottomless pools, immured adulteresses and talking animals' *London Review of Books*

'Wonderful . . . Contains almost every myth, legend and ghost story ever told in England' Simon Hoggart, *Guardian*

# PENGUIN SCIENCE

**IN SEARCH OF THE MULTIVERSE**
JOHN GRIBBIN

*In Search of The Multiverse* takes us on an extraordinary journey, examining the most fundamental questions in science. What are the boundaries of our Universe? Can there be different physical laws to the ones we know? Are there in fact other universes? Do we really live in a Multiverse?

This book is a search – the ultimate search – exploring the frontiers of reality. Ideas that were once science fiction have now come to dominate modern physics. And, as John Gribbin shows, there is increasing evidence that there really is more to the Universe than we can see. Gribbin guides us through the different competing theories revealing what they have in common and what we can come to expect.

Along the way Gribbin explores the very latest thinking about quantum theory, about gravity and the fundamental forces that shape our world, about time and multiple dimensions, about matter itself, and the growth and fate of the known Universe.

John Gribbin is our best, most accessible guide to the big questions of science. And there is no bigger question than our search for the Multiverse.